Authors

Andrew Murray was born in South Africa in 1828. After receiving his education in Scotland and Holland, he returned to South Africa and spent many years there as both pastor and missionary. He was a staunch advocate of biblical Christianity. He is best known for his many devotional books.

Charles Finney was born in 1792, and trained as a lawyer before becoming one of America's foremost evangelists. Over half a million people were converted under his ministry in an age that offered neither amplifiers nor mass communication tools. He served as Professor of Theology and President of Oberlin College in Ohio.

L. G. Parkhurst, Jr., is a pastor who has compiled and edited several devotional classics from such writers as John Bunyan, Charles Finney, Andrew Murray and Edith Schaeffer. He currently resides in Rochester, Minnesota.

Books by Andrew Murray

ANDREW MURRAY CHRISTIAN MATURITY LIBRARY

The Believer's Absolute Surrender
The Believer's Call to Commitment
The Believer's Full Blessing of Pentecost
The Believer's New Covenant
The Believer's New Life
The Believer's Prophet, Priest and King
The Believer's Secret of a Perfect Heart
The Believer's Secret of Christian Love
The Believer's Secret of Holiness
The Believer's Secret of Living Like Christ
The Believer's Secret of Obedience
The Believer's Secret of Spiritual Power
The Believer's Secret of the Master's Indwelling
The Spirit of Christ

ANDREW MURRAY PRAYER LIBRARY

The Believer's Prayer Life
The Believer's School of Prayer
The Ministry of Intercessory Prayer
The Secret of Believing Prayer

ANDREW MURRAY DEVOTIONAL LIBRARY

The Believer's Daily Renewal
The Believer's Secret of Intercession
The Believer's Secret of the Abiding Presence
The Believer's Secret of Waiting on God
Day by Day with Andrew Murray

How to Raise Your Children for Christ
Revival

Contents

Introduction

Compiling and editing this new book in the Andrew Murray Christian Maturity Library series was a deeply moving spiritual experience for me. As I worked through the daily devotions of Andrew Murray and then divided the articles and tracts of Charles Finney into companion pieces, I was amazed at how complementary each one's book is. For me, it was as though these two books had been meant to be brought together at some point in time.

As you read through these devotions, I hope you will be struck, as I was, with how each man emphasized two important aspects of the work of the Holy Spirit in our lives. Though Andrew Murray titled his book *The Secret of Power from on High*, his primary concern was our bearing the *fruits* of the Holy Spirit in our daily lives. Charles Finney's collection of articles and tracts was titled *Power from on High*, but his primary concern was the *gifts* of the Holy Spirit. Charles Finney's thoughts follow Murray's thoughts in this book under the subheading "The Practice of Spiritual Power."

Even more surprising than this balance between the fruits of the Spirit and the gifts of the Spirit is that Murray and Finney lay down the same conditions for receiving the power from on high that makes sharing these fruits and gifts possible.

You will find books by Charles Finney and Andrew Murray are clear, practical guides to spiritual power. There are many to choose from that are published by Bethany House and other publishers.

This book follows my *The Believer's Secret of the Abiding Presence*. In that book I combined books by Andrew Murray and Brother Lawrence into a thirty-one day devotional. Both books conclude each devotional with a prayer that I have written which reflects my own meditation upon the text. I hope you will find these prayers helpful as you begin your own personal prayers to God each day.

This book may also introduce readers of Andrew Murray to Charles Finney for the first time, or Charles Finney readers to Andrew Murray for the first time. Should you like to read more devotionals from Charles Finney's works, I suggest *Answers to Prayer*, which illustrates what the enduement of power from on high can do in a person's life, *Principles of Prayer* and *Principles of Union with Christ*, all published by Bethany House. Finney's sermons and lectures on prayer can be found in *Principles of Devotion*, also published by Bethany House. I hope, in the coming months, to prepare more Andrew Murray devotionals combining his work with other authors. There are many writers of devotionals from the 17th through the 19th centuries who have much to share, and perhaps through Andrew Murray they can be introduced to 20th-century readers. I hope these books introduce many to the classic devotional works designed to lead us into a closer walk with Jesus Christ in the power of the Holy Spirit.

With love in the Lamb,
L. G. Parkhurst, Jr.

*H*ow much more will
your Father in heaven give
the Holy Spirit to those who
ask Him?

Luke 11:13

1

The Dispensation of the Spirit

*T*he author of a concise book on prayer writes that he has learned through experience the secret of a better prayer life, and would gladly pass on that which has helped him. While meditating on prayer, he was deeply moved by the great thought that we are presently living in the dispensation of the Holy Spirit. He writes, "I felt deeply that in this time of the working of the Holy Spirit, all we may do in God's service is of little value unless it is inspired by the power of the Holy Spirit. This brought me to the well-known, precious and inexhaustible text, 'How much more will your Father in heaven give the Holy Spirit to those that ask Him?' "

His thoughts reflect this teaching: the thing for each of us is to receive afresh from the Father the Holy Spirit for our daily needs and daily life. Without the Holy Spirit we cannot please God, nor can we be of any real help to our neighbors. And this brings the further thought that our prayers, if they are to raise our lives to fulfill God's purpose, must have their origin in God himself, the highest source of power.

Water cannot rise higher than its source. So, if the Holy Spirit prays through us, as human channels or conduits, our prayers will rise to God, Who is their source, and the prayers will be answered by the Divine working in ourselves and in others. "I believe more and more," says the writer, "that the Christian life of each one of us depends chiefly on the quality of our prayers and not on the quantity."

What food for thought, for deep meditation and earnest prayer! When you pray today, ask the Heavenly Father to give you the Holy Spirit afresh for this day. He yearns to do it.

Father, grant me *now* the working of your Holy Spirit that I may learn to pray.

The Practice of Spiritual Power

The mission of the Church is to disciple all nations. Christ gave the Great Commission to the *whole* Church. Every member of the Church is under obligation to make it his lifework to convert the world.

To have success in this great work, we need the enduement of power from on high. Christ informed the disciples that without Him they could do nothing. When He gave them the commission to convert the world, He added, "But tarry ye in Jerusalem till ye be endued with power from on high. Ye shall be baptized with the Holy Spirit not many days hence. Lo, I send you the promise of My Father." The baptism of the Holy Spirit as promised by the Father, the enduement of power from on high, Christ specifically informed us is the indispensable condition of performing the work which He has given us.

Christ expressly promised the baptism of the Holy Spirit to the whole Church, and to every individual whose duty it is to labor for the conversion of the world. Until they had received this enduement of power from on high, He admonished the first disciples not to undertake the work. Both the promise and the admonition apply equally to all Christians of every age and nation.

No one has any right at any time to expect success, until he receives this enduement of power from on high. The example of the first disciples teaches us how to receive it. They first *consecrated themselves* to this work, continuing in prayer and supplication, until the Holy Spirit fell upon them on the Day of Pentecost, filling them with the promised power from on high. This, then, is the way to receive it.

*D*ear Father, thank you for sending your Son into the world to save sinners. Thank you, dear Jesus, for sending me into the world to further carry out your great purpose. I consecrate myself totally to doing your will in your way, that an untold number might see in my life and hear in my words a true witness to your saving power. I cannot carry on your work without the spiritual power which only your indwelling Holy Spirit can provide. Endue me with power from on high each day, that I might succeed in fulfilling the Great Commission, because you are doing your work within me. Amen.

*T*he fruit of the Spirit is
love, joy, peace, patience,
kindness, goodness,
faithfulness, gentleness and
self-control.

Galatians 5:22, 23

2
The Fruit of the Spirit

We have seen the first two lessons on prayer: the first is that we pray to the Father every morning to give us the Holy Spirit anew, and second that we then pray to the Holy Spirit to teach us and help us. Here is a third lesson: commit to memory the text at the beginning of this devotional.

Christians often think that they only have to ask God to teach them to pray, and He will do it immediately. This is not always the case. Instead, the Holy Spirit strengthens our spiritual lives so we are able to pray better.

When we ask Him to teach us, it is important that we open our hearts to His gracious influence, so that our desires are stirred and we first of all surrender ourselves to the working of the Holy Spirit. This surrender consists in naming before Him the fruits of the Spirit with the earnest prayer to be filled with these fruits. So the benefit of learning the text by heart will be that as we pray for the teaching of the Holy Spirit, we may pray, "Here is my heart. Fill it with the fruits of the Spirit."

Think of the first three fruits: *love, joy, peace*. These

three are the chief characteristics of a strong life of faith. *Love* to God the Father and to Jesus Christ, to our brothers and sisters in the faith, and to all people. *Joy* is the visible proof of the perfect fulfillment of your every need, of courage and faith for all the work we have to do. God's *peace* is the blessed state of undisturbed rest and security for our hearts and minds that passes all understanding.

In Jesus' last discourse with His disciples, He used these three words with the word *My* before them: "Abide in *My love*"; "*That My joy* might remain in you"; "*My peace* I give unto you." Shall we not petition the Holy Spirit as the great desire of our hearts that He may make these fruits reach perfection within us? Then at last we shall be able to pray rightly, and always ask more and more of our Heavenly Father.

The Practice of Spiritual Power

The Father is more willing to give us the Holy Spirit than we are willing to give good gifts to our own children. From Scripture we learn how infinitely easy it is to obtain the Holy Spirit, this enduement of power from the Father.

Receiving spiritual power must be a constant subject of prayer. Everyone seems to pray for more power all the time. Yet, with all this intercession, very few, comparatively, are really endued with this spirit of power from on high. The lack of power is a subject of constant complaint. Christ said, "Everyone that asketh receiveth," but there certainly is a great gulf between the asking and the receiving. This has brought confusion to many.

If you do not receive spiritual power from on high, God has a good reason for not granting your request. Sometimes we are unwilling, on the whole, to have what we desire or ask. God has specifically told us that if we regard iniquity in

16

our hearts He will not hear us. If we are self-indulgent, this is iniquity, and God will not hear us. If we are uncharitable or censorious or self-dependent, we cannot receive divine power. If we refuse conviction of sin, refuse to confess our sins to those concerned, refuse to make restitution to injured parties, then God will not fill us with His Holy Spirit. A person who is prejudiced, uncandid, resentful or revengeful cannot receive the baptism of the Holy Spirit. Those with worldly ambitions cannot have spiritual power to achieve their selfish aims.

If you have committed yourself to some point, and have become dishonest, and neglect and reject further truth, then God cannot give you power from on high. If you profess yourself a believer, but are denominationally selfish, selfish for your own congregation and resisting the teachings of the Holy Spirit, God cannot trust you with spiritual power. You must not grieve the Holy Spirit by persistence in justifying wrong, grieve Him by a lack of preparedness or resist Him by indulging evil tempers. In your everyday life, if you are dishonest in business, indolent, negligent in business, study, or prayer, selfish, impatient in waiting upon the Lord or undertake too much business, study or prayer, God will not grant you His promised blessing.

You must consecrate yourself entirely to God, and not be guilty of unbelief. If you pray for spiritual power and do not expect to receive it, then "he that believeth not God, hath made Him a liar." This is the greatest sin of all. What an insult, what a blasphemy, to accuse God of lying!

*D*ear Jesus, if I lack spiritual power in my life, then the fault is not yours but mine. I confess that too often I have not wanted to bear the true fruits of the Spirit. I have wanted spiritual power for selfish reasons. Throughout the days ahead, I pray that your Holy Spirit would reveal to me any unconfessed sins in my life or any unbiblical lifestyle, that I might remove any obstacles to the cleansing presence and power of your Holy Spirit in my life. Help me to live a life worthy of your shed blood. Amen.

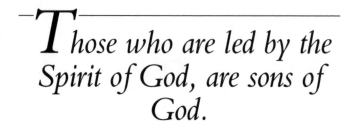

Those who are led by the Spirit of God, are sons of God.

Romans 8:14

3
Led by the Spirit

*L*et us now consider four other fruits of the Holy Spirit: *long-suffering, gentleness, goodness, meekness.* Each of these four words denotes an attribute of God. They will reach maturity in us through much prayer for the working of the Holy Spirit in our lives. Look at how God uses them to draw people to himself.

Long-suffering. Scripture bears witness to the wonderful *patience* God has toward sinners. The Word of God says in 2 Peter 3:9, "The Lord is long-suffering, not willing that any should perish, but that all should come to repentance." The Holy Spirit will make this attribute of God a blessed characteristic of our lives, so that we too may exercise a divine patience with all sinners and wrongdoers in order that they may be saved.

Gentleness. What wonderful things we read in the Psalms about God's goodness and gentleness, which are from everlasting to everlasting. "As the heaven is high above the earth, so great is his mercy toward them that fear him." God works in our hearts this same goodness and mercy in dealing with all the sin and wretchedness around us.

Goodness. Jesus taught, "There is none good but God." All goodness comes from Him, and He gives to His children according to what each heart asks and desires. And this goodness is manifested in sympathy and love to all who are in need.

Meekness. We read in Psalm 18:35, "Thy gentleness hath made me great." But divine meekness was shown chiefly in God's only begotten Son. Jesus taught, "Learn of me, for I am meek and lowly in heart." Paul entreated his readers "by the meekness and gentleness of Christ." The Holy Spirit appeared to Jesus as the gentle dove. The Holy Spirit longs to impart the ripe fruit of meekness to our hearts.

It is a wonderful thought that these four attributes of God, which are the characteristics of God's work among sinners, may be brought to ripeness in our hearts by the Holy Spirit, so that we in all our ways and conversation may be like the Meek and Lowly One.

The Practice of Spiritual Power

Persistent sin in our lives explains why we receive so little from God. However, if we ask and fulfill the plainly revealed conditions of prevailing prayer, then with certainty we shall receive the promised enduement of power from on high, and we will be successful in winning souls for Christ.

There is a great difference between the *peace* and the power of the Holy Spirit in the soul. The disciples were believers before the Day of Pentecost, and as such they had a measure of the Holy Spirit. They must have had the peace of sins forgiven, and the peace of a justified state, but they did not have the enduement of power necessary to accomplish the work Jesus had assigned them. They had the *peace* which Christ had given them, but not the *power* which He had promised.

Having *peace* but no *power* may be true of many Christians. The great mistake of the Church and of the ministry is that we stop at conversion, rather than seeking until this enduement of power from on high is obtained. Hence, so many who profess to be believers have no power with either God or man. They prevail with neither. They cling to a hope in Christ, and even enter the ministry, overlooking the admonition to wait until they are endued with power from on high. But let anyone bring all the tithes and offerings into God's treasury, let him lay all upon the altar, and he shall find that God "will open the windows of heaven, and pour him out a blessing that there shall not be room enough to receive it."

Do you earnestly seek the power from on high?

*D*ear Father, I lay all that I am and all that I have at your feet. Thank you for receiving me as I am through the cleansing power of the blood of Jesus. Help me to have a closer relationship with you through the presence of your Spirit in my life. I do not desire to exercise raw, untamed spiritual power to impress those around me; but I desire it to bring glory to your name. Transform my life completely that I might manifest the fruits of your Spirit for the salvation of souls through Christ. Amen.

With that same spirit of faith we also believe.

2 Corinthians 4:13

4
The Spirit of Faith

Do you realize why it is so important to commit to memory the text in Galatians 5:22–23, "The fruit of the Spirit is love, joy, peace, long-suffering, gentleness, goodness, faith, meekness, temperance"? Learning this text by heart, and committing yourself to bearing these fruits in the power of the Holy Spirit will strengthen the desire in your heart to have and to hold the fruits of the Spirit within you. Our expectation of the blessing God can give will be enlarged. Let us pause awhile on the two last fruits of the Spirit: *faith* and *temperance.*

When the disciples asked the Lord, "Why could we not cast out the evil spirit?" He replied, "This kind goeth not out but by prayer and fasting." Their faith was not powerful enough, and even if they had prayed they had not the zeal and self-sacrifice needed for prevailing prayer. Here we see the union of faith and temperance.

Faith is a fruit of the Spirit. Faith leads the seeking soul to depend on God alone. Faith believes God's Word, clings to Him, and waits in perfect trust that His power will work within us everything that He has promised. The whole life

25

of the believer is a life of faith.

Let us now think of *temperance*. Temperance refers in the first place to eating and drinking. Temperance leads us to restraint, carefulness, and unselfishness in our conversation, our desires, and in all our fellowship with one another. Our motto should be: "Forsaking all worldly desires, to live righteously and godly and temperately in all things." We must use temperance in all our dealings with the world and its temptations; righteousness in the doing of God's will. We must be devout in our close communion with God himself.

Faith and temperance are both fruits of the Spirit. When we ask the Holy Spirit to teach us to pray, we open our hearts toward Him that He might grant us both of these along with the other fruits of the Spirit, to influence our daily lives in our relationship with God and others.

Learn this text by heart and let the promptings of the Holy Spirit in your heart each day lead you to the Father, that He may grant the fruits of the Spirit in your inner life, which will be seen in all your actions.

The Practice of Spiritual Power

The apostles exercised great power after the Day of Pentecost. They received a powerful baptism of the Holy Spirit, a vast increase of divine illumination. This baptism imparted a great diversity of gifts that were used for the accomplishment of their work.

The baptism of the Holy Spirit gave them *the power of a holy life*. The power of a self-sacrificing life. The power of a cross-bearing life. The power of great meekness. The power of a loving enthusiasm in proclaiming the gospel. The power of a loving and living faith. The gift of tongues. An increase of power to work miracles. The gift of inspiration, or the revelation of many truths before unrecognized by them. The power of moral courage to proclaim the gospel and do the bidding of Christ whatever the cost. The manifestation of these gifts must have had a great impact on those to whom they proclaimed the gospel.

In their circumstances, all these enduements were essential to their success. But neither separately nor all together did they constitute that power from on high which Christ promised and which they manifestly received. The essential means of success was the power to prevail with God and man, the power to convict the minds of men. This was the promise of Christ the disciples had waited for. Christ had commisssioned the Church to convert the world to Him. All the other gifts named above were only means, which could never secure that end unless they were vitalized by the power of God. The apostles, doubtless, understood this. Leaving themselves and their all upon the altar, they beseiged the Throne of Grace in the spirit of entire consecration to their work.

*D*ear Jesus, I earnestly desire the fruits of the Holy Spirit to be manifest in my relationships with others. I pray they will be effective in bringing many into a saving relationship with you. Lord, the natural powers that I have are woefully inadequate to perform the spiritual work you have called me to do. I pray for many powerful baptisms of the Holy Spirit, so I can do your work in a way that will bring many people to you for a full salvation. Amen.

We are the true circumcision, who worship God in spirit, and glory in Christ Jesus, and put no confidence in the flesh.

Philippians 3:3

5

Worship God in the Spirit

*O*ur text prepares us for prayer itself. We have come to the Father with the prayer for the Holy Spirit. We have invoked the guidance of the Holy Spirit. Now we begin to pray.

First, we pray to God the Father, thanking Him for all the blessings of this life. We acknowledge our entire dependence and powerlessness, and express our trust in His love and care for us. We wait before Him until we have the assurance that He sees and hears us. Then we direct our prayer to the Lord Jesus, and ask for grace to abide in Him always, for without Him we can do nothing. We look to Him as our Lord, our Preserver, our Life, and give ourselves into His keeping for the day. We express our faith in His infinite love, and the reality of His presence with us.

Finally, we pray to the Holy Spirit. We have already prayed to Him for guidance. We now ask Him to strengthen us in the faith, that what we have asked of the Father and the Son may be truly forged in us. The Holy

Spirit is the Dispenser of the power and gifts of the Father and of the Lord Jesus. All the grace we need must be the result of the working of the Spirit within us.

Our text says that we serve God in the spirit. We must glory in the Lord Jesus, and have no confidence in the flesh. We have no power to do the thing that is good. We count on the Lord Jesus, through the Holy Spirit, to work within us. Let us take time to think and meditate on these things. It will help to strengthen our faith if we repeat the text of Galatians 5:22–23, "The fruit of the Spirit is love, joy, peace, long-suffering, gentleness, goodness, faith, meekness, temperance," asking God to grant these fruits in our lives. As we surrender ourselves wholly, we shall have boldness by faith to accept the working of the Holy Spirit in our hearts.

The Practice of Spiritual Power

The power from on high is supremely and principally given to bring people to salvation. When the Lord Jesus gave the apostles a powerful baptism of the Holy Spirit, it was immediately manifested. They began to address the multitude, and wonderful to tell, three thousand were converted the same hour. But, observe, there was no new power manifested by them upon this occasion except the gift of tongues. They worked no miracle at that time, and used these tongues simply as the means of making themselves understood by the foreign multitudes.

Note that the apostles had not had time on the Day of Pentecost to exhibit any other gifts of the Spirit. They had not at that time the advantage of exhibiting a holy life or any of the powerful graces and gifts of the Holy Spirit. What was said on the occasion, as recorded in the Scriptures, could not have made the saving impression upon the people that it did had it not been uttered by them with a new power.

The power manifest at Pentecost was not the power of inspiration, for they only declared certain facts of their own knowledge. It was not the power of human learning and culture, for they had but little. It was not the power of human eloquence, for there appears to have been but little of it. It was God speaking in and through them. It was a power from on high—God in them making a saving impression upon those to whom they spoke.

This power to savingly impress abode with them and upon them. It was, doubtless, the great and main thing promised by Christ and received by the apostles and the early believers. It has existed, to a greater or less extent, in the Church ever since. It is often manifest in a most surprising manner. Sometimes a single sentence, a word, a gesture, or even a look, will convey this power in an overwhelming way.

Are you willing to lay all upon the altar, to receive a mighty baptism of the Holy Spirit, so as to become a powerful and effective witness for Christ?

Dear Father, thank you for hearing my prayers in the name of your Son. I desire with all my heart to do His will now and always—His good, pleasing and perfect will. I long to witness powerfully in His name. Anoint me with the Holy Spirit again and again that I might be able to do this. Guide me into all the truth, that I might know you more completely and share the truth more effectively for Jesus' sake. Amen.

Pray for each other.

James 5:16

6
Intercession

*T*here is much value in intercession, and it is an indispensable part of prayer. It strengthens love and faith in what God can do, and is a means of bringing blessing and salvation to others. Learn the lesson thoroughly: Prayer should not be for yourself only, but chiefly for others. Begin by praying for those who are near and dear to you, those with whom you live, that you may be of help to them and not a hindrance. Pray for divine wisdom, for thoughtfulness toward others, for kindness, for self-sacrifice on their behalf.

Pray for all your friends and all with whom you come in contact. Pray that you may be reminded to watch in prayer for their souls. Pray for all Christians, especially for ministers and those in responsible positions.

Pray for those who do not yet know the Lord as their Savior. Make a list of the names of those whom God has laid upon your heart and pray for their conversion. You belong to Christ. He needs you to bring to Him in prayer the souls of those around you. The Holy Spirit will strengthen you to an active love in watching for souls. Pray, too, for all poor and neglected people.

Pray for the heathen and for all mission work. Use a mission calendar, with daily subjects of prayer, and bear on your heart before God the missionaries, evangelists, teachers, and believers among the heathen.

Do you think this will take too much time? Just think what an inconceivable blessing it is to help souls through your prayers, and look to the Holy Spirit for further guidance. If this takes too much time in your morning watch, then take some time later in the day. Cultivate the attitude: *I am saved to serve!* You will taste the great joy of knowing that you are living even as Jesus Christ lived on earth—to make God's love known to others.

The Practice of Spiritual Power

To the honor of God alone I will say a little about my own experience in this matter. I was powerfully converted on the morning of the 10th of October. In the evening of the same day, and on the morning of the following day, I received overwhelming baptisms of the Holy Spirit. These baptisms went through me, as it seemed to me, body and soul.

I immediately found myself endued with such power from on high that a few words dropped here and there to certain people were the means of their immediate conversion. My words seemed to fasten like barbed arrows in the souls of men. They cut like a sword. They broke the heart like a hammer. Multitudes can attest to this. Oftentimes a mere word would fasten conviction, and often result in almost immediate conversion.

Sometimes I would find myself, in a great measure, empty of this power. I would go out and visit, and find that I had no convicting power; would exhort and pray, with the same result. I would then set apart a day for private fasting and prayer, fearing that this power had departed from me, and would inquire anxiously after the reason of this apparent emptiness. After humbling myself, and crying out for help, the power would return upon me with all its freshness. This has been the experience of my life.

Dear Father, I confess that I have not had the love for others that I need to have, that I am commanded to have. I have not spent time seeking their conversion as I ought. But worse than this, O Father, I confess that I have not loved you as I should. My lack of love is apparent in the very little time I spend in concentrated prayer and reading of your Word. If I truly loved you, then time spent in fasting and prayer would be one of my greatest delights. Father, truly sanctify my heart with your Spirit, that I might see my salvation as a calling not just to eternal life, but a calling to love and serve you forever. Amen.

Could you men not keep watch with Me for one hour?

Matthew 26:40

7
Time

One who wishes to pray as we have indicated in our previous meditations might say, "I think I could do all that in ten minutes of time." Very well, if ten minutes is all the time that you can give, see what you can do in that time. Most people can spare more time. If they will only persevere from day to day, with their hearts set on prayer, time will come of its own accord.

It is sad that believers say they cannot afford to spend a quarter or half an hour alone with God and His Word. Yet, when a friend comes to visit or an important meeting comes up, or something for the believer's advantage or pleasure, time is found easily enough.

But God, the great God, who in His wondrous love longs for all to spend time with Him, that He may communicate His power and grace—no time is found for fellowship with Him. Even God's own servants, who might consider it their special privilege to be much with Him in prayer to receive the fullness of power—even His servants are so occupied with their own work that they find little time for that which is all-important—waiting on God to receive power from on high.

Dear child of God, never say, "I have no time for God." Let the Holy Spirit teach you that the most important, the most blessed, the most profitable time of the whole day is the time we spend alone with God. Pray to the Lord Jesus, who in His earthly life experienced the need of prayer. Pray to the Holy Spirit, who will impress upon us this divine truth. Communion with God through His Word and prayer is as indispensable to you as the bread you eat and the air you breathe.

Whatever else is left undone, God has the first and chief right to your time. Then only will your surrender to God's will be full and unreserved.

The Practice of Spiritual Power

I have hope for the usefulness of a person who, at any cost, will keep up daily fellowship with God; who is yearning for and struggling after the highest possible spiritual attainment; who will not live without daily prevalence in prayer and being clothed with power from on high.

Believers should know of the power of Christ to save from sin, know of the power of prayer, and whether and to what extent they are endued with spiritual power to win souls to Christ.

Decide now and forever to hold fast to the promise of Christ and never think yourself or anyone else fit for the great work of the Church until you have received a rich enduement of power from on high.

I beseech you to more thoroughly consider this matter, to wake up and lay it to heart, and rest not until this subject of the enduement of power from on high is brought forward into its proper place and takes that prominent and practical position in view of the whole Church that Christ designed it should. Spend time in prayer daily, that you might be of use to God and a faithful servant in His kingdom, that His power might work mightily within you.

*L*ord Jesus, why are we believers so guilty of not praying with you even one hour. Help me to pray consistently for that power from on high as a means to bring others to you. Help me to so walk with you that being my constant companion will make a difference in the lives of those who have no regard for your presence. Amen.

The Word of God is living and active.

Hebrews 4:12

8
The Word of God

I find it a great help to use much of God's Word in my prayers. If the Holy Spirit impresses a certain text upon my mind, I take it to the throne of grace and plead the promise. This habit increases our faith, reminds us of God's promises, and brings us into harmony with God's will. We learn to pray according to God's will, and understand that we can only expect an answer when our prayers are in accordance with that will. The Apostle John wrote, "And this is the confidence that we have in Him, that, if we ask any thing according to His will, He heareth us" (1 John 5:14).

Prayer is like fire. The fire can only burn brightly if it is supplied with good fuel. That fuel is God's Word, which must not only be studied carefully and prayerfully, but must be taken into the heart and lived out in the life. The inspiration and powerful working of the Holy Spirit alone can do this.

By thoughts such as these, we gain a deeper insight into the value and power of God's Word as a seed of eternal life. We are all familiar with the characteristics of a seed—

a small grain in which the life-power of a whole tree slumbers. If it is placed in the soil it will grow and increase and become a large tree.

Each word or promise of God is a seed containing a divine life in it. If I carry it in my heart by faith, love it and meditate on it, it will slowly and surely spring up, bringing forth the fruits of righteousness. Think over this until you gain the assurance: *Although my heart seems cold and dead, the Word of God will work within me the disposition promised in His Word.*

The Holy Spirit uses both the Word and prayer. Prayer is the expression of our human need and desire. The Word of God is the means that the Holy Spirit uses to teach us what God will do for us, and the demonstration of the secret working of the Holy Spirit in our hearts, by which God himself fulfills His promise and gives us what we could not obtain without the help of the Spirit.

The Practice of Spiritual Power

The power from on high is a great marvel. When the preaching has been anointed by the Holy Spirit in answer to prayer, many times I have seen people unable to endure the Word of God. The most simple and ordinary statements would cut them off from their seats like a sword, would take away their bodily strength, and render them almost as helpless as dead men. Their conscience would convict them of the truth of God's Word.

Several times it has been true in my experience that I could not raise my voice in preaching, or say anything in prayer or exhortation except in the mildest manner, without wholly overcoming those that were present. This was not because I was preaching terror to the people, but the sweetest sounds of the gospel in the Word of God would overcome them. The Holy Spirit would bring the Word to their hearts with the power to convict them.

This power from on high sometimes seems to pervade the atmosphere of anyone who is highly charged with the Holy Spirit and the Word of God. Many times great numbers of people in a community will be clothed with this power, when the very atmosphere of the whole place seems to be charged with the life of God. Strangers coming into the community, and passing through the place, will be instantly smitten with conviction of sin, and in many instances converted to Christ.

When Christians humble themselves and consecrate their all afresh to Christ, and ask for this power, they will often receive such a baptism that they will be instrumental in converting more souls in one day than in all their lifetime before. While Christians remain humble enough to retain this power, the work of conversion will go on, till whole communities and regions of the country are converted to Christ.

*D*ear God, I love your Word. The psalmist loved your Word so much that he meditated upon it day and night. Help me understand the promises of your Word and how they can apply to my life today. Fill me with your Holy Spirit, so that I can share your Word with the wisdom and power to lead others to saving faith in you. I long more than anything to be able to convert more people to Christ. Use me in any way that you wish, and help me to remain humble so you can get the glory for all that you do through me and so I can remain a worthy vessel for the outpouring of your power and grace. For Jesus' sake. Amen.

Whatever you do, whether in word or deed, do it in the name of the Lord Jesus, giving thanks to God the Father through him.

Colossians 3:17

9
In the Name of Christ

At the close of your prayers it is always well to add a request for the "Spirit of Remembrance," who "shall bring all things to your remembrance" all through the day. You must make this request so the prayers of the morning may not be counteracted by the work of the day.

Have you ever realized that these words of Scripture, "Whatsoever ye do, in word or in deed, do all in the name of the Lord Jesus, giving thanks to God the Father through Him," are a command? Is it the aim of your life to obey this command? Do you sincerely desire to fulfill its injunction? This may be difficult, but it is not impossible or God would not have commanded us to do it.

God's Word has a wonderful power to preserve the spirit of thanksgiving in our lives. When we rise in the morning, let us "in the name of the Lord Jesus" thank God for the sleep we had. In His name, let us at night thank Him for the mercies of the day. The ordinary daily life, full of most ordinary duties, will thus be lightened by the thought of what God has done for us for Christ's sake. Each ordinary deed will lead to thankfulness that He has given us the power to perform it.

At first, it may seem impossible to remember the Lord Jesus in everything and to do all in His name. Yet, the mere endeavor will strengthen us. Even as a mother is conscious of her love for her child all through the day's hard work, so the love of Christ will enable us to live all day in His presence. We need to completely surrender ourselves—to live for God all the day.

I have often spoken and written of what it means to pray in the name of Jesus Christ. On reading our text of today, I thought: Here we have the right explanation. The man who does all in word and deed in the name of Jesus may have the full childlike confidence that what he asks in that name, he will receive. Take the text into your heart, and you may count on the Holy Spirit to make it true to your life.

The Practice of Spiritual Power

You will receive whatever you ask in prayer, if you fulfill the conditions that God has set forth for answering prayer.

Unselfishness. "Ye ask and receive not because ye ask amiss, that ye may consume it upon your lusts" (James 4:3).

A conscience void of offense toward God and man. "If our heart (conscience) condemn us, God is greater than our heart and knoweth all things; if our heart condemn us not, then have we confidence toward God, and whatsoever we ask we receive of Him, because we keep his commandments and do those things that are pleasing in his sight" (1 John 3:20, 21). Here two things are made plain: first, that to prevail with God we must keep a clear conscience; and second, that we must keep His commandments and do those things that are pleasing in His sight.

A pure heart. "If I regard iniquity in my heart, the Lord will not hear me" (Psalm 66:18).

All due confession and restitution to God and man. "He that covereth his sins shall not prosper. Whoso confesseth and forsaketh them shall find mercy" (Proverbs 28:13).

Clean hands. "I will wash mine hands in innocency, so will I compass thine altar, O Lord" (Psalm 26:6). "I will therefore that men pray everywhere, lifting up holy hands, without wrath and doubting" (1 Timothy 2:8).

The settling of disputes and animosities among brethren. "If thou bring thy gift to the altar, and there rememberest that thy brother hath aught against thee, leave there thy gift before the altar and go thy way; First be reconciled to thy brother, and then come and offer thy gift" (Matthew 5:23, 24).

Humility. "God resists the proud, but giveth grace to the humble" (James 4:6).

Taking up the stumbling blocks. "Son of man, these men have set up their idols in their heart, and put the stumbling block of their iniquity before their face. Should I be inquired of at all by them?" (Ezekiel 14:3).

A forgiving heart. "Forgive us our debts as we forgive our debtors. . . . But if we forgive not men their trespasses, neither will your Father forgive your trespasses" (Matthew 6:12, 15).

The exercise of a truthful spirit. "Behold, thou desireth truth in the inward parts" (Psalm 51:6).

Praying in the name of Christ. "Whatsoever ye shall ask in my name, that will I do that the Father may be glorified in the Son" (John 14:12).

Dear Father God, renew my mind with your Word and Spirit to help me to view the everyday things of this life through the eyes of your Son. Impress upon my spirit the necessity of lifting these things before you in prayer with the personal commitment to make a difference where needed. Be with me all the day that I might not be discouraged beyond relief, but encouraged through the remembrance that you answer prayer for the sake of those you love in Jesus. Amen.

He will glorify me, for he
will take what is mine, and
declare it to you.

John 16:14

10
The Spirit Glorifies Christ

To understand the work of the Holy Spirit and to truly experience it, you must try to grasp the relationship of the Holy Spirit to the Lord Jesus Christ. Before His departure, our Lord said that the Holy Spirit would come as a Comforter to His disciples. *The Holy Spirit would reveal Christ to them in all His heavenly glory.* Although He and His disciples would be apart for awhile, they would soon be together in a very special way. This made the disciples pray earnestly for the Holy Spirit, for they longed to have Jesus with them always. This was the promise of their Master: *the Spirit would reveal Him to them.*

This is the meaning of our text: "The Spirit shall glorify me"—even as I am in the glory of heaven, the Holy Spirit will make Me known. "He shall take of mine"—My love, My joy, My peace, and all My life, and "reveal it unto you." When we have an earnest desire for the glory of Jesus in our lives, the Holy Spirit will respond, preserving the holy presence of Jesus in our hearts all the day.

We must quietly endeavor day in and day out to abide in fellowship with Christ, to love Him and keep His commandments, and do all things in His name. Then we will be able to count upon the secret and powerful working of the Holy Spirit within us.

We see again and again the value of remembering and meditating on the text in Galatians 5:22–23, "The fruit of the Spirit is love, joy, peace, long-suffering, gentleness, goodness, faith, meekness, temperance." If our thoughts are always occupied with the Lord Jesus—His love, His joy, His peace—then the Holy Spirit will graciously ripen these fruits within us.

The great desire of the Holy Spirit and of the Father is that Christ may be glorified in and through us. Let it be the earnest desire and prayer of our lives too!

The Practice of Spiritual Power

The true nature of faith does not consist in any degree of mere intellectual knowledge or acceptance of the doctrines of the Bible. The firmest possible persuasion that every word said in the Bible respecting God and Christ is true is not faith.

Faith is firmly trusting in God and committing our lives to Him by placing all our confidence in Him for all that He is affirmed to be to us in the Bible. We trust Christ upon the testimony of God in the Bible. We trust Him for what the doctrines and facts of the Bible declare Him to be to us. This act of trust unites our spirit to Him in a union so close that we directly receive from Him a current of eternal life. Faith, in consciousness, completes the divine salvation plan, and the life of God is instantly imparted to our souls. God's life, light, love, peace and joy seem to flow to us as naturally and spontaneously as the electric current from a battery.

Then, for the first time, we understand what Christ meant by our being united to Him by faith, as the branch is united to the vine. Christ is then revealed to us as God. We are conscious of direct communion with Him. We know Him by His direct activity within us. We then know directly, in consciousness, that He is our life, and that we receive from Him, moment by moment, an impartation of eternal life.

With some the mind is comparatively dark, and their faith, therefore, comparatively weak in its first exercise. Hence, their trust in Him will be as narrow as their convictions. When faith is weak, the current of the divine life will flow so mildly that we are scarcely conscious of it. But when faith is strong and all-embracing, it lets a current of the divine life of love into our souls so strong that it seems to permeate both soul and body. We then know in consciousness what it is to have Christ's Spirit within us as a power to save us from sin and keep us on the path of loving obedience.

Love the Scriptures intensely because they testify of Jesus. True faith will inspire you to search and devour the Scriptures intensely because they tell you who Jesus is and what you may trust Him for. Those who are truly saved go directly to Christ by an act of loving trust and thus join their souls to Him in a union that receives from Him, by a direct divine communication, the things for which they are led to trust Him. This is saving faith.

*D*ear Lord, I am overwhelmed when I think of what you do in and with those who maintain a daily moment-by-moment relationship with you. Help me to know you so well, as I learn more about you, that I recognize your presence with me. Help me to feel the deep satisfaction the apostles must have felt when you replaced your physical presence with them by sending your Spirit to indwell them. I pray for your daily presence and power from on high so I can serve you in ways that will bring many to love you and praise you for your work in their own lives. Amen.

Pray in the Holy Spirit.
Keep yourself in God's love.

Jude 20, 21

11
Praying in the Spirit

Paul began the last section of the epistle to the Ephesians with the words: "Be strong in the Lord and the power of His might." He speaks of the whole armor of God, and closes by saying that this armor must be put on with prayer and supplication, "praying always in the Spirit." As the believer needs to be strong in the Lord all the day, and to wear his armor against the foe the whole day, so he needs to live always praying in the Spirit.

The Holy Spirit desires this, wanting to be with us more often than just at certain times when we think we need His aid. The Spirit comes to be our life-companion. He wants us wholly in His possession at all times; otherwise, He cannot do His work in us. Many Christians do not understand this. They want the Spirit to help and to teach them, but do not grasp the truth that He must dwell in them continually and have full possession of all their being.

When this truth is grasped, we will realize that it is possible to live always "praying in the Holy Spirit." By faith we will have the assurance that the Spirit will keep us in a prayerful attitude, and make us realize God's presence, so that our prayer will be the continual exercise of fellowship with God and His great love. But as long as we regard the work of the Holy Spirit as restricted to certain times and seasons, it will remain an unsolved mystery and a possible stone of offense.

Jude expressed the same thought as the Apostle Paul when he wrote, "Praying in the Holy Spirit, keep yourselves in the love of God." This is what each child of God desires, and what the Holy Spirit will do within him—keep him in the love of God, even as I may keep in the sunlight all day long. It is this blessed nearness of God which can enable me to abide in His love at all times, even in the busiest moments of my life, praying without ceasing, entirely dependent on Him.

The Practice of Spiritual Power

As we pray always in the Holy Spirit, all the day long, consciously realizing the continual presence of the living God in our hearts, there are many things that we need to pray and do to be prepared to share the gospel of Christ with others.

See that you are motivated by love to share the gospel with others. Contemplate much the guilt and danger of sinners, that your zeal for their salvation may be intensified. Also deeply ponder and dwell much upon the boundless love and compassion of Christ for them. So love them yourself as to be willing to die for them. Give your most intense prayerful thoughts to the study of ways and means by which you may save sinners. Make this the great and intense study of your life.

Be sure that you have the special enduement of power from on high through the baptism of the Holy Spirit. See that your heart as well as your head is committed to sharing the gospel. Develop a hearty and most intense inclination to seek the salvation of souls as the great work of life. Constantly maintain a close walk with God. Make the Bible your book of books. Study it much, upon your knees in prayer, waiting for divine light. Keep yourself pure—in will, in thought, in feeling, in word and action.

Believe the assertion of Christ that He is with you in this world always and everywhere to give you all the help you need, especially in the work of sharing the gospel. "He that winneth souls is wise." "If any man lack wisdom, let him ask of God, who giveth to all men liberally and unbraideth not, and he shall receive." "But let him ask in faith." Remember, therefore, that you are obligated to have the wisdom that shall win souls to Christ. The gospel is adapted to change the hearts of people, and in a wise presentation of it, you may expect the efficient cooperation of the Holy Spirit. Being called of God to the work, make your calling your constant argument with God for all that you need for the accomplishment of the work.

Teach others by example as well as by precept. Practice yourself whatever you preach or teach. Let simplicity, sincerity, and Christian propriety stamp your whole life. Spend much time every day and night in prayer and direct communion with God. This will make you a power for salvation. No amount of learning and study can compensate for the loss of this communion. If you fail to maintain communion with God, you are "weak as another man." See that you personally know and draw your life from Christ.

Dear Father, I long to make every moment count for you as I serve others in your name. Help me to remember that as I maintain moment by moment fellowship with you that you will anoint me with the power I need to bear witness of your love for everyone. Amen.

Don't you know that you yourselves are God's temple and that God's Spirit lives in you? . . . God's temple is sacred and you are that.

1 Corinthians 3:16, 17

12
The Temple of God

*F*rom eternity it was God's desire for man to be a dwelling in which to show forth His glory. Because of our sin this plan was a seeming failure. But through His people Israel, God sought a means of carrying out His plan. He would have a house in the midst of His people—first a tabernacle and then a temple—in which He could dwell. This was but a shadow and image of the true indwelling of God in redeemed mankind, who would be His temple to eternity. We are built up "into a holy temple, for a habitation of God through the Spirit" (Ephesians 2:22).

Since the Holy Spirit has been poured forth, He has His dwelling in each heart that has been cleansed and renewed by the Spirit. The message comes to each believer, however feeble he may be: "Know ye not that ye are a temple of God?" How little this truth is known or experienced. And yet how true it is, "The temple of God is holy, which temple ye are."

Paul testified of himself, "Christ liveth in me." This is the fullness of the gospel which he preached: the riches of the glory of the mystery, Christ in you. This is what he prayed for so earnestly for believers, that God would strengthen them through His Spirit in the inner man, that Christ might dwell in their hearts by faith.

Yes, this is what our Lord himself promised: "If a man loves me, he will keep my words and my Father will love him, and *we will come unto him, and make our abode with him.*" It is strange that believers are so slow to receive and adore this wonder of grace.

It is through the Holy Spirit that you will be sanctified into a temple of God, and you will experience that Christ, with the Father, will take up His abode in your heart. He will do it on this one condition, that you surrender yourself wholly to His guidance.

The Practice of Spiritual Power

A truly successful soul winner must not only win souls to Christ, but must keep them won. He must not only secure their conversion, but their permanent sanctification. Nothing in the Bible is more expressly promised in this life than *permanent sanctification.* Paul wrote and prayed, "The very God of peace sanctify you wholly; and I pray God your whole spirit, soul, and body be preserved blameless unto the coming of our Lord Jesus Christ. Faithful is he that calleth you, who also will do it" (1 Thessalonians 5:23, 24). This is unquestionably a prayer of the apostle for permanent sanctification in this life, with an express promise that He who has called will do it.

We learn from the Scriptures that "*after* we believe" we are, or may be, *sealed* with the Holy Spirit of promise. Paul explained, "In whom ye also trusted after that ye heard the word of truth, the gospel of your salvation; in whom also after that ye believed, ye were sealed with that Holy Spirit of promise, which is the earnest of our inheritance until the redemption of the purchased possession, unto the praise of his glory" (Ephesians 1:13, 14). This sealing, this downpayment of our inheritance, renders our salvation sure. Hence, the apostle warns, "Grieve not the Holy Spirit of God, whereby ye are sealed unto the day of redemption" (Ephesians 4:30). To the Corinthians he wrote, "Now he which established us with you in Christ, and hath anointed us, is God, who hath also sealed us and given the earnest of the Spirit, in our hearts" (2 Corinthians 1:21, 22). Thus we are *established* in Christ and *anointed* by the Spirit, and also *sealed* by the *earnest* of the Spirit in our hearts. This is a blessing that we receive after we believe. Now, it is extremely important to receive by faith in Christ to teach converts this *permanent sanctification*, this sealing, this being established in Christ by the special anointing of the Holy Spirit. Unless we know what this means by our own experience, and lead converts to this experience, we fail most lamentably and essentially in our teaching. We leave out the fullness of the gospel.

Permanent sanctification consists in entire and permanent consecration to God, and implies the refusal to obey the desires of the flesh or of the mind. Sin consists in carnal-mindedness, "obeying the desires of the flesh and of the mind." The baptism or sealing of the Holy Spirit subdues the power of our desires. Offer your whole being to God, consecrate yourself to His service, abide permanently in the presence of Christ, and the Holy Spirit will empower you to live a holy and Christlike life.

Dear Father, thank you for making my body into your holy temple. I offer my body to you as a living sacrifice. Use me according to your will for the accomplishment of your purposes. Amen.

*T*he fellowship of the Holy Spirit be with you.

2 Corinthians 13:14

13
The Fellowship of the Spirit

*I*n this verse we have one of the chief character-istics and activities of the Holy Spirit. It is the Holy Spirit through whom the Father and the Son are one, and through whom they have fellowship with each other in the Godhead. For the Holy Spirit is the true life of the Godhead.

We have fellowship with the Father and the Son through the Spirit: "Our fellowship is with the Father and the Son." "Hereby know we that He abideth in us, by the Spirit which He has given us" (1 John 3:24). Through the Spirit we know and experience the fellowship of love with the Father and the Son.

Through the Holy Spirit we, as God's children, have fellowship with one another. The child of God should have nothing of the selfishness and self-interest that seeks its own welfare supremely. We are members of one Body. "It is one Body and one Spirit." Through the Spirit the unity of the Body can be maintained.

One reason the Holy Spirit does not work with

greater power in the Church is that the unity of the Spirit is too little sought after. At Pentecost, after ten days spent in united prayer, the one hundred and twenty seemed melted together into one. They received the Spirit in fellowship with one another.

We have fellowship in the bread and wine when we meet at the communion table. We also have fellowship one with another in the trials of other members of the Body. Always it is: "The fellowship of the Spirit be with you now and evermore." Remember the words in Galatians about the fruits of the Spirit; present them to the Spirit in prayer, and so make manifest your love for all God's children.

In heaven there is an eternal fellowship of love between Father and Son through the Spirit. Do you really long to be filled with the Spirit? Offer yourself to God. Beseech Him to grant you the unity and the fellowship of the Spirit with all members of Christ's Body.

The Practice of Spiritual Power

Certain conditions must be fulfilled before you can receive the enduement of power from on high. This is seen in the lives of the disciples in the last chapters of Matthew and Luke regarding the great commission, and the first and second chapters of the Acts of the Apostles.

Before Pentecost the disciples had already been converted to Christ, and their faith had been confirmed by His resurrection. But conversion to Christ is not to be confused with a consecration to the great work of the world's conversion. In true conversion, the soul yields up its prejudices, its antagonisms, its self-righteousness, its unbelief, its selfishness, and accepts Christ, trusts Him, and supremely loves Him. All this the disciples had, more or less, distinctly done. But as yet they had received no definite commission, and no particular enduement of power from on high to fulfill a commission.

But when Christ had dispelled their great bewilderment, resulting from His crucifixion, and confirmed their faith by repeated interviews with them, He gave them their great commission to win all nations to himself. And then, He admonished them to tarry in Jerusalem, until they received power from on high, which He promised they would receive.

Now observe what they did. The men and the women assembled for prayer and fellowship. They accepted the commission, and doubtless came to an understanding of the nature of the commission and the necessity of the spiritual power Christ had promised.

As they continued in prayer and fellowship, they no doubt came to understand the difficulties before them and their inadequacy to do the task. May your sense of inadequacy encourage you to seek all that Christ would give you. Seek the fellowship and encouragement of other Christians desiring to fulfill Christ's commission. Your difficulties are opportunities for God to work in your life in varied ways through the indwelling Holy Spirit. Consecrate yourself wholly to Christ and ask Him for that promised power from on high.

Dear Father, I am amazed at what you can do through a few consecrated, Spirit filled people. I am grateful that through your Word and through the testimony of those who have preached your Word in the power of the Spirit, we can see your wonderful mercy extended to the vilest of sinners. May I be one of those who out of love prays diligently for the lost, seeking a way for them to hear the gospel and receive Christ in faith. Amen.

You will seek Me, and
find Me when you seek Me
with all your heart.

Jeremiah 29:13

14
With the Whole Heart

You have often heard it said that if you seek to perform any great work, you must do it *with your whole heart and with all your powers*. In worldly affairs this is the secret of success and victory. The same is true in divine things, it is indispensable, especially in praying for the Holy Spirit.

The Holy Spirit desires to have full possession of you. If He is to show His full power in your life, He will be satisfied with nothing less. He has the right. Why? Because He is the Almighty God.

Have you ever realized when you pray for the Holy Spirit *that you are praying for the whole Godhead to take possession of you*? Do you really understand this? Or have your prayers had a wrong motive? Do you want the Holy Spirit's power, but not the Holy Spirit's call on your life? That would be a great mistake. The Holy Spirit must have *full* possession.

You say, that is just the trouble. You do not feel such a burning, urgent desire, and you do not see any chance of its becoming true in your life. God knows about this weakness of yours. He has ordained in His divine providence that the Holy Spirit shall work within you all you need. What God commands and demands of us, *He will himself work within us.* On our part there must be the earnest prayer to the Father each day and an acceptance of the Holy Spirit as our leader and guide.

Child of God, the Holy Spirit longs to possess you wholly. Take time to give Him your answer, and cast yourself in complete dependence on the word of His promise, and on His almighty power at work within you.

The Practice of Spiritual Power

During the disciples' prayer meeting in the upper room, prior to their baptism in the Holy Spirit on the Day of Pentecost, they consecrated themselves to the conversion of the world as their life work. They must have utterly renounced the idea of living for themselves in any form, and devoted themselves with all their powers to the work set before them.

This consecration of themselves to the work, this self-renunciation, this dying to all that the world could offer them, must, in the order of nature, have preceded their seeking of the promised enduement of power from on high.

They continued, with one accord, in prayer for the promised baptism of the Holy Spirit, a baptism essential for their success. Observe. They had a work set before them. They had a promise of power to perform it. They were admonished to wait until the promise was fulfilled.

How did they wait?

Not in listlessness and inactivity. Not in making preparations by study. Not by going about their business and offering occasional prayer that the promise might be ful-

fulled. They *continued* in prayer. They *persisted* in the pursuit until the answer came. They understood that it was to be a baptism of the Holy Spirit. They understood that it was to be received from Christ. They prayed in faith. They held on, with the firmest expectation, until the power came.

Now in the days ahead, may these facts instruct you as to the conditions of receiving this enduement of power.

Dear Lord, I do desire to be used by you for the conversion of the world, the fulfillment of the great commission. I desire that you possess me wholly, and I commit my will to knowing and doing your perfect will. I commit my life and work to whatever you will for me to do. I pray that your Holy Spirit would be my guide, my protector, my friend and my strength. I know that I am truly converted and wholly consecrated. Endue me with power from on high that I might be used far beyond my own expectations. Amen.

God has poured out his love into our hearts by the Holy Spirit, whom he has given us.

Romans 5:5

_15_
The Love of God in Our Hearts

*T*he Holy Spirit is shed abroad in our hearts by God the Father. The love of God is shed abroad in our hearts through the Holy Spirit. As truly as God has poured forth the Spirit, so truly is the love of God shed forth by the Spirit.

Why do we so seldom experience this? The answer is simple: unbelief. It takes time to believe in the mighty working of the Holy Spirit through whom our hearts are filled with the love of God. We need time away from the world and its interests, and time alone basking in the light of God so that His love may take possession of our hearts.

If we believe in the infinite love of God, and the divine power with which He takes possession of the heart, then we will receive what we ask for—*the love of God shed abroad in our hearts by the Holy Spirit.* God desires His children to love Him with all their hearts and all their strength. He knows how weak we are. And for that very reason He has given the Spirit, who searches the deep things of God, and in these depths has found the fountain of eternal love available to fill our hearts.

If you long for this, draw nigh to God, and abide with Him in quiet worship and adoration, and you will come to know the love of God in Christ which passes all knowledge.

The Holy Spirit wants you to have this. He will teach you each day to dwell with the Father in His great love to abide in the love of Christ, and to express that love toward the brethren and toward a perishing world. He will make your heart a fountain of everlasting love, springing up to life eternal and flowing forth in blessing to all around. Say with a heart full of thanksgiving, "The love of God is shed abroad in my heart through the Holy Spirit."

The Practice of Spiritual Power

The Bible specifically teaches that sin is overcome by faith in Christ: "[He] is made unto us wisdom, and righteousness, and sanctification, and redemption." "[He] is the way, the truth, and the life." Believers are told to "purify their hearts by faith." In Romans 9:31–32, it is affirmed that the Jews did not obtain righteousness, "because they sought it not by faith, but as it were by the works of the law."

The doctrine of the Bible is that Christ saves His people from sin through faith; that Christ's Spirit is received by faith to dwell in the heart. It is faith that works by love. Love is wrought and sustained by faith. By faith, Christians "overcome the world, the flesh, and the devil." It is by faith that they "quench all the fiery darts of the wicked." It is by faith that they "put on the Lord Jesus Christ, and put off the old man, with his deeds." It is by faith that we "stand," by resolutions we fall. This is the victory that overcometh the world, even our faith.

It is by faith that the flesh is kept under and carnal desires subdued, and by faith that we receive the Spirit of Christ to work in us to will and to do, according to His good pleasure. He sheds abroad His own love in our hearts, and thereby enkindles ours. Every victory over sin is by faith in Christ. Whenever the mind is diverted from Christ, by resolving and fighting against sin, whether we are aware of it or not, we are acting in our own strength, rejecting the help of Christ, and are under a specious delusion. Nothing but the life and energy of the Spirit of Christ can save us from sin, and trust is the universal condition for the working of His saving energy within us.

How deep rooted in the heart of man is self-righteousness and self-dependence? So deep that one of the hardest lessons for the human heart to learn is to renounce self-dependence and trust wholly in Christ. When we open the door by implicit trust, He enters in and takes up His abode with us and in us. By shedding abroad His love, He quickens our souls into sympathy with himself, and in this way, and in this way alone, He purifies our hearts through faith. He sustains our will in the attitude of devotion. He quickens and regulates our affections, desires, appetites and passions, and becomes our sanctification.

Lord Jesus, thank you for the promise that whatever I do for you I do not do alone. Endue me with the power from on high, the powerful inner working of your Holy Spirit so we can work together in the power of your strength. Inspire me to be persistent in my prayers for continual baptisms of your Holy Spirit. Amen.

*L*ive by the Spirit . . .
since we live by the Spirit,
let us keep in step with the
Spirit.

Galatians 5:16, 25

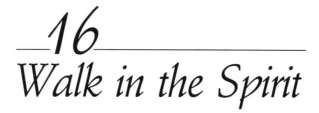

16
Walk in the Spirit

*T*he word "walk" reminds us of daily life with our fellowman. The Christian in his walk and conversation must follow the leading of the Spirit and walk by the Spirit. Walking by the Spirit will be the sign of the spiritual man, who serves God in the Spirit and does not trust in the flesh.

People speak as though the Spirit were only needed in our conversation with God when we pray, or for our work in the service of His kingdom. This is a great mistake. God gives us His Spirit to be in us the whole day. We need Him most in the midst of our daily work, because the world has such power to lead us away from God. We need to pray to the Father every morning for a fresh portion of His Spirit for each day. During the course of the day let us remind ourselves that the Spirit is with us, and lift up our hearts to God, remembering that the Spirit abides with us always.

Paul wrote, "As ye have received Christ Jesus our Lord, so walk ye in Him"; and again, "Put on the Lord Jesus Christ." As I put on my coat when I go out, so the

Christian must put on the Lord Jesus and show by his conduct that Christ lives in him and that he walks by the Spirit.

"Walk in the Spirit, and ye shall not fulfill the lusts of the flesh." As long as we are not under the guidance of the Holy Spirit, the flesh will rule over us. Oh, that we knew the unspeakable value of the grace God has given! The Spirit of His Son in our hearts will cry "Abba, Father," so that we may walk the whole day in God's presence as His beloved children. Christian, learn this lesson. *The Holy Spirit is given you to teach you that you may walk by the Spirit at all times.* Thank God continually for His divine leader, who gives us daily renewal from heaven and enables us to walk and to abide in Christ.

The Practice of Spiritual Power

We, as Christians, have the same commission to fulfill as the first disciples. As truly as they did, we need an enduement of power from on high. Of course, the same injunction to wait upon God until we receive spiritual power is given to us.

We have the same promise that the early disciples had. Now, let us take the same course they took. They were Christians and had a measure of the Holy Spirit to lead them in prayer and consecration. So have we, if we are truly Christians. Every Christian possesses a measure of the Spirit of Christ, enough of the Holy Spirit to lead them to true consecration and inspire them with the faith that is essential to their prevailing in prayer.

Let us, then, not grieve or resist the Spirit of Christ, but accept the commission and fully consecrate ourselves with all that we have to the saving of souls as our great and only life work. Let us get on the altar, dedicating all we have and are, and stay there, persisting in prayer until we receive the enduement of power.

Now, observe, conversion to Christ is not to be confused with the acceptance of the great commission to convert the world. The first is a personal transaction between the person and Christ relating to his salvation. The second is the person's acceptance of the work Christ has for the believer. Christ does not require us to make bricks without straw. To whom He gives the commission, He also gives the admonition and the promise. If the commission is heartily accepted, if the promise is believed, if the admonition is complied with, if we wait upon the Lord until our strength is renewed by the Holy Spirit, we shall receive the enduement of power from on high.

*D*ear Father, I do accept the great commission that you have given to all Christians, and I consecrate all that I am and have to the growth of your kingdom. I wait now for the filling of the Holy Spirit to give me the spiritual power I need to be an effective witness for you right now where I am, and I am open to going wherever you might lead for Jesus' cause. Amen.

If you love Me, you will obey what I command. And I will pray the Father, and He will give you another Counselor.

John 14:15, 16

17

The Spirit Promised to the Obedient

Christ would ascend to heaven and pray to the Father to send the Comforter, the Holy Spirit. He would not only do this once, but it would form part of His intercessory work. He would remain "ever living to make intercession." The continual communication of the Spirit of the Father with us comes through the Son.

The Lord tells us here on what conditions He will send the Holy Spirit. If we love Him and keep His commandments, "I will pray the Father." This is a word of deep meaning, a searching word—a word of greatly needed and blessed teaching. The Holy Spirit is given so we can do the will of the Father. The condition is reasonable and just, that as far as we have kept the commandments through the Spirit, the Spirit will be granted to us in fuller measure. As we heartily accept this truth, and yield ourselves willingly to the Spirit's guidance, we shall receive from day to day the fullness of the Spirit. Let us say to God that we accept the condition with all our heart, and will strive to keep His commands, and ask for power to do His commandments more perfectly.

Do not listen to the whispers of Satan or give way to unbelief and sloth. Surrender yourself unreservedly to the Lord, Who has said, "If you love Me, you will keep My commands." Love will enable you to do it. The Lord Jesus does not deceive us with a vain hope in this matter. No, He gives the grace, He gives His own love in our hearts, teaching us to say, "I delight to do Thy will."

Let us trust Him with childlike faith, and give ourselves wholly—that is all that is necessary—to do His will. Then the beauty of the divine agreement that He makes with us will dawn upon us, "If ye keep My commandments ye shall abide in My love," and the Father will send the Holy Spirit anew each day.

The Practice of Spiritual Power

It is of the utmost importance that all Christians understand that the great commission to convert the world is given to them by Christ *individually*.

Everyone has the great responsibility to win as many people as possible to Christ. This is the great privilege and the great duty of all disciples of Christ. There are many positions in this work; and in each one the Church ought to possess this spiritual power, that, whether we preach, pray, write, print, trade, travel, take care of children or administer the government of the state or whatever we do, our whole life and influence should be permeated with spiritual power.

Christ says, "He that believeth on Me, as the Scripture hath said, out of his belly shall flow rivers of living water." Christ means that the power to impress the truth of God upon the hearts of others shall proceed from His Spirit in us.

The great lack of the Church at present is, first, the conviction that this commission to convert the world is given to each of Christ's disciples as his *individual* life work. I fear I must say that the great mass of people professing to be believers seem never to have been impressed with this truth. The work of saving souls is something they feel they can leave to ministers.

The second great lack is the conviction that the enduement of spiritual power is a necessity for every believer. Many believers suppose it belongs only to those who are called to preach the gospel as a life work. They fail to realize that all are called to preach the gospel, that the whole life of every believer is to be a proclamation of the glad tidings.

*D*ear Jesus, help me to convince others that your spiritual power is available to them if they would only believe and obey, and that you expect them to be involved in the conversion of the world. Use me to convict them of disobedience, if they try to pass off their obligation on others, and show my friends that spiritual power is not only a joy to receive but a necessity if they are to live the true Christian life that influences others. Amen.

Brothers, I could not address you as spiritual but as worldly—mere infants in Christ.

1 Corinthians 3:1

18
Spiritual or Carnal?

*I*n 1 Corinthians, Paul describes the three spiritual conditions of man. There is *the natural man* in his unconverted state—one who cannot "receive the things of the Spirit of God" (1 Corinthians 2:14); there is *the spiritual man*, who "can discern spiritual things" (1 Corinthians 2:13, 14); and between the two there is *the carnal man* who is called a "babe in Christ" and who lives in jealousy and strife (1 Corinthians 3:3). The carnal Christian is one who makes room for sin in his life.

However, God calls us, and the Spirit draws us to be spiritual men and women—that is to say, people who pray each day to be led and guided into a truly spiritual life free from the power of sin.

When the Lord Jesus promised the Spirit to His disciples, it was in the full expectation that they *would yield themselves wholly to the leading and power of the Holy Spirit.* And the condition is the same now as it was then. The Holy Spirit will be granted anew each day, if we yield ourselves unreservedly to His sanctifying power. Oh, that our eyes were open to see how right and how blessed this is!

Many believers pray for the Holy Spirit, but always with a certain reservation, still intending to maintain a hold over certain parts of their lives. Oh, Christian, when you pray, entrust yourself fully to the guidance of the Holy Spirit for the whole day. If there is a true willingness on your part, then the Holy Spirit will take full possession of you, and will preserve and sanctify your life. Do not serve God half-heartedly. Pray for the enlightenment of the Holy Spirit, that you may see the possibility and the blessedness of a life wholly surrendered to His service.

The Practice of Spiritual Power

Too many Christians do not believe Christ's promise that He would endue the Church with spiritual power; they doubt that His promise is to *every* believer. Consequently, they have no faith to lay hold of Christ's power. If His promise does not belong to *all*, how can they know to whom it does belong? Of course, with this limited understanding they cannot lay hold of the promise by faith.

Another lack in Christians is *persistence* in waiting upon God for that which He has promised to us in the Scriptures. People give up before they have prevailed, and hence, the enduement of spiritual power is not received.

Of great concern also is the extent to which the Church has practically lost sight of the necessity of the enduement of spiritual power. Much is said about our dependence upon the Holy Spirit by almost everybody, but how little is this dependence realized. Christians and even ministers go to work without any spiritual power. I mourn to be obliged to say that the ranks of the ministry seem to be filling up with those who do not possess spiritual power. May the Lord have mercy upon us! Will this last remark be thought uncharitable? If so, let the current state of the

Church and her success in evangelism be heard on this subject. Surely, something is wrong.

Dear God, I do not want to be a mere spiritual baby needing milk instead of meat. I feast on your Word and desire to know the deeper meanings of what I read. I do not seek this knowledge as an end in itself, but to know you fully as Lord and Friend. Help me grow to spiritual adulthood, fill me with power so that I might help others grow. Amen.

*T*he glorious Father, may give you the Spirit of wisdom and revelation, so that you may know Him better. I pray also that the eyes of your heart may be enlightened.

Ephesians 1:17, 18

19
The Spirit of Wisdom

*I*n the Word of God we find a wonderful combination of the human and the divine. The language is that of a man. Anyone who has a good understanding can grasp the meaning of the words and the truths contained in God's Word. Yet this is all that man, in the power of his human understanding, can do.

There is a divine side in which the Holy God expresses His deepest thoughts to us. The carnal man cannot attain to them, or comprehend them, for they must be "spiritually discerned." Only through the Holy Spirit can the believer appropriate the divine truth contained in God's Word.

Paul prays earnestly that God would grant the spirit of wisdom to his readers, eyes that are enlightened through the Holy Spirit to understand what is written and to know the exceeding greatness of His power working in all who believe.

Much of our religion is ineffectual, because people accept the truths of God's Word with the intellect and strive to put them into practice in their own strength, but *it is only the Holy Spirit who can reveal divine truth to us.* A young student in a theological seminary may accept the truths of God's Word as head knowledge, while the Word has little power in his heart to grant him a life of joy and peace in the Lord Jesus.

Paul teaches that when we read God's Word, or meditate on it, we should pray, *Father, grant me the Spirit of wisdom and revelation.* As we do this each day we will find that God's Word is living and powerful, and will work change in our hearts. God's commands will be changed into promises. His commands are not grievous and the Holy Spirit will teach us to do lovingly and joyfully all that He has commanded.

The Practice of Spiritual Power

Look at current statistics on the work of the Church as a whole. How many are being saved? How many are being lost to the world? How many are doing their duty? How many are fully consecrated to Christ and His will? How many are manifesting spiritual power in their work for God? The reported facts certainly indicate a most alarming weakness among believers.

Have all, or even a majority of Christians or even ministers, been endued with the power which Christ has promised? If not, why not? But, if they have, are they demonstrating all that Christ intended by His promise?

There are many devoted and self-denying laborers in the cause of God. But statistics illustrate the alarming weakness that pervades every branch of the Church, both clergy and laity. Are we not weak? Are we not *criminally* weak? It has been suggested that by writing as I have, I offend the ministry and the Church. I cannot believe that statements so obviously true will be regarded as an offense.

The fact is, there is something sadly defective in the education of the ministry and of the Church. The ministry is weak because the Church is weak. And then again, the Church is kept weak by the weakness of the ministry. Oh, for a conviction of the necessity of this enduement of power and faith in the promise of Christ!

Earlier I said that the reception of this enduement of spiritual power is instantaneous. I do not mean to assert that in every instance the recipient was aware of the precise time at which the power began to work mightily within him; it may have started like the dew and increased to a shower. But however it is received, where the Holy Spirit is at work there is power to do the work of God according to His will for the blessing of many in the Church and the salvation of souls.

Dear Father, I do weep when I think of the state of the Church today. We are so weak, and it seems that in the battle for souls the world is winning more than the gospel. I do not complain of you and your work, Father, but the Church lacks spiritual wisdom and spiritual power because ministers and laity are unwilling to do their duty—labor for the conversion of the world. Grant me your wisdom and power, anoint devoted and self-denying Christians everywhere, so the Church can be awakened to its true condition and be saved from the judgment she deserves for her faithlessness and powerlessness. Amen.

Who have been chosen according to the foreknowledge of God the Father, for obedience to Jesus Christ and sprinkling by His blood.

1 Peter 1:2

20
The Spirit of Sanctification

*I*n the Old Testament God was revealed as the thrice-holy One. The Spirit is mentioned more than a hundred times, but only three times as the Holy Spirit. But in the New Testament, the word *holy* is regularly ascribed to the Holy Spirit, and Christ sanctified himself for us that we might be holy. The great work of the Holy Spirit is to glorify Christ in us as our sanctification.

Has this truth ever taken hold of you—in your church prayer meetings or in your private devotions—that the great object for which the Holy Spirit is given is to sanctify you? If you do not accept this truth, the Holy Spirit cannot do His purifying work. If you only want the Spirit to help you to be a little better, and to pray a little more, you will not get very far. But when you once understand that He has the name of *Holy* Spirit in order to definitely impart God's holiness and that He will sanctify you wholly, then you will begin to realize that the Holy Spirit dwells in your heart.

And what will be the result? You will feel that He must have you wholly. He must rule and control the whole day. Your life and conversation must be in the Spirit. Your prayer, faith, and fellowship with the Father and all work in God's service must be completely under His sway. As the Spirit of holiness, He is the Spirit of sanctification.

Dear friends, what I have just said is deep eternal truth. Even if we are willing to accept this truth and meditate on it daily, it will be of no avail if we do not wait upon God to grant us the Spirit of heavenly wisdom and a vision of what God has intended for us in His wonderful gift—the Spirit of sanctification. Each morning say slowly and calmly, *"Abba, Father, for this new day renew within me the gift of Thy Holy Spirit."*

The Practice of Spiritual Power

The lack of enduement of power from on high should be deemed a disqualification for a pastor, a deacon or an elder, a Sunday School superintendent, a professor in a Christian college, and especially for a professor in a theological seminary. Is this a hard saying? Is this an uncharitable saying? Is it unjust? Is it unreasonable? Is it unscriptural?

Suppose any one of the apostles, or any of those present on the Day of Pentecost, had failed through apathy, selfishness, unbelief, indolence, or ignorance to obtain this enduement of spiritual power. Would it have been uncharitable, unjust, unreasonable or unscriptural to have accounted him unqualified for the work which Christ had appointed him? If he was not wholly committed to the work of Christ, could he have performed the required service?

Christ had specifically informed them that without

this enduement they could do nothing. He had expressly told them not to even attempt it in their own strength, but to wait at Jerusalem until they received the necessary power from on high. He had also promised that if they waited, in the sense which He intended, they would receive it "not many days hence." They committed themselves to obeying their risen Lord by waiting and praying.

Now, suppose that any one of them had stayed away and attended to his own business and waited for the sovereignty of God to confer this power. He, of course, would have been disqualified for the work. And if his fellow believers, who had obtained the power, had deemed him disqualified, would it have been uncharitable, unreasonable and unscriptural? No. The Holy Spirit was promised to equip them for the work of Christ. The Holy Spirit was promised to empower believers and make them pure vessels of Christ's love for others. When believers give themselves wholly to the work of Christ, they will experience the power of the Holy Spirit at work in them. They will not be disqualified.

*D*ear Father, thank you for showing me that sanctification, the living of a holy life, can only be done as I maintain a moment-by-moment relationship with your Holy Spirit. Thank you for helping me see the riches of your grace for this life as well as the next. I do wait with prayerful expectation for the enduement of spiritual power before I perform any task for you—I cannot succeed in my own strength. In Jesus' name I pray. Amen.

*Whoever believes in Me,
as the Scripture has said,
streams of living water will
flow within him.*

John 7:38

21
Rivers of Living Water

Our Lord in His conversation with the Samaritan woman said, "The water that I shall give him shall be in him a well of water springing up into everlasting life." In our text the promise is even greater: rivers of living waters flowing from Him, bringing life and blessing to others.

John says further that this refers to the Holy Spirit, Who was to come when Christ had been glorified, for the Holy Spirit was not yet poured out. The Spirit of God was mentioned in the Old Testament, but the Holy Spirit had not yet been given. Before He could pour out the Holy Spirit into the hearts of His followers, Christ first had to be offered on the cross through the eternal Spirit and raised from the dead by the Spirit of holiness, and receive from the Father power to send forth the Holy Spirit. Scripture testifies, "How much more shall the blood of Christ, who through the eternal Spirit, offered himself without spot to God, purge your conscience from dead works to serve the living God" and He was "declared to be the Son of God with power, according to the spirit of holiness, by the resurrection of the dead" (Hebrews 9:14 and Romans 1:4). Only through the victory of Christ over death can the Christian say: *Now the Holy Spirit of Christ is in me.*

In order to experience these two wonderful promises of the well of water and the rivers of living water, the believer must give up the right to run his own life, he must have *the inner attachment to Christ, the unreserved surrender to fellowship with Him, and the firm assurance that the Holy Spirit will work in him what he cannot do.* Christ put it much more simply, *He that believeth in Me.* Faith is needed that rejoices in the divine might and love, and depends on Him day by day so that living water may flow forth.

If the water from a reservoir is to flow into a house all day, one thing is necessary—the connection must be perfect, then the water passes through the pipe of its own accord. So the union between you and Christ must be uninterrupted. Your faith must accept Christ and depend on Him to sustain your new life.

Let your faith rejoice that Jesus Christ gives us the Holy Spirit, and may you have the assurance that the Holy Spirit is within you as a fountain of blessing.

The Practice of Spiritual Power

Every believer has been given the command to disciple the world and has the promise of the power from on high. If through any shortcoming or fault of your own you fail to obtain the gift of the Holy Spirit, you are in fact disqualified for the work of the Church and especially for any official position within the Church.

If you have not received the baptism of the Holy Spirit can you be qualified for leadership, to be a teacher or preacher? If it is a fact that you lack spiritual power, however this defect is to be accounted for, it is also a fact that you are not qualified to be a teacher of God's people. If you are seen to be discredited because you lack spiritual power, it must be reasonable and right and scriptural for the Church to deem you unqualified, and so to speak to you, and so to treat you.

Who has a right to complain? Surely, you have not. Shall the Church of God be burdened with teachers and leaders who lack this fundamental qualification, when their failing to possess it must be their own fault? The manifest apathy, indolence, ignorance and unbelief that exist upon this subject are truly amazing. If you do not have the power from on high, you are inexcusable. You must be highly criminal. With such a command to convert the world ringing in your ears, with such an injunction to wait in constant, wrestling prayer until you receive power, with such a promise of all the help you need held out to you by such a Savior as Jesus Christ, what excuse can you offer for being powerless in the work? What an awful responsibility rests upon you, upon the whole Church, upon every Christian!

One might ask, how is apathy, how is indolence, how is the common fatal neglect of the Holy Spirit's power possible under such considerations?

*D*ear Father, you promised me that I would experience the presence and power of your Holy Spirit in my life as a "river of living water." Thank you for making possible such a wonderful experience of spiritual power. I love you. Help me to pray and reach out to those who need these rivers of blessing in their own lives. Should there be any who are trusting to make your will and way known to others, may I prayerfully and actively support them in this gospel ministry in the Name of Jesus. Amen.

*F*or the kingdom of God is righteousness and peace and joy in the Holy Spirit. May the God of hope fill you with all joy and peace as you trust in him by the power of the Holy Spirit.

Romans 14:17; 15:13

22

Joy in God

A believer said to me shortly after his conversion, "I always thought that if I became religious it would be impossible for me to do my worldly business. The two things seemed so contrary. I seemed to be a man trying to dig a vineyard with a bag of sand on his shoulders. But when I found the Lord, I was so filled with joy that I could do my work cheerfully from morning till night. The bag of sand was gone; the joy of the Lord was my strength for all my work." Truly a significant lesson.

Many Christians do not understand that the joy of the Lord will keep them and equip them for their work. Even slaves, when filled with the love of Christ, could testify to the happiness that He gave them.

Read the two texts given. See how the kingdom of God is pure joy and peace *through* the Holy Spirit, and how God will "fill us with all joy and peace in believing . . . *through the power of the Holy Spirit.*" Then try to realize that the Holy Spirit will give this joy and peace of Christ in our hearts. To many the thought of the Holy Spirit is a matter of grief and self-reproach, of desire and disappointment, of something too high and holy for them. What a foolish thought, that the great gift of the Father, meant to keep us in the joy and peace of Christ, should be a matter of self-reproach and worry!

Remember Galatians 5:22, "The fruit of the Spirit is love, joy, peace, long-suffering, gentleness, goodness, faith, meekness, temperance." Listen attentively to the voice of the Spirit each day as He points to Jesus Christ, who offers you this wonderful fruit: *"My love, My joy, My peace."* "In whom, though now ye see Him not, yet believing, ye rejoice with joy unspeakable and full of glory" (1 Peter 1:8).

Pray in all humility to the Holy Spirit, believing firmly that He will lead you into the joy of the Lord.

The Practice of Spiritual Power

The attitude and experience of numerous professing Christians is lamentable and amazing, since the Bible is in their hands. Many appear satisfied with theological *opinions* they more or less firmly hold. This they believe to be faith. Others go a little further, but only wind up with a conviction as to what the Bible says concerning Christ. Others have strong impressions about the obligations of the law, leading them to a life of works which leads them to bondage. They pray from a sense of duty; they are dutiful, but not loving, not confiding. They have no peace and no rest, except in cases where they persuade themselves that they have done their duty. They are in a restless, agonizing state:

> *Reason they hear, her counsels weigh,*
> *And all her words approve,*
> *And yet they find it hard to obey,*
> *And harder still to love.*

102

They read and perhaps search the Scriptures to learn their duty and to learn about Christ. They intellectually believe all that they understand the Scriptures to say about Him; but they do not so join their souls to Him as to receive from Him the influx of His life, light and love. They do not by a simple act of personal loving trust in His person receive the current of His divine life and power into their own souls. Thus they do not take hold of His strength and interlock their being with His. In other words, they do not truly believe. Hence, they are not saved. Their psychology of faith is mistaken; mere intellectual conviction of the truth of the gospel is not faith.

Let all know that I value the facts and doctrines of the gospel. I regard a knowledge and belief of them as of fundamental importance. I have no sympathy with those who treat doctrinal discussion and preaching as of minor importance. Nor can I assent to the teaching of those who would have us preach Christ and not the doctrines of the Bible that teach us who Christ is, why He is to be trusted, and for what. How can we preach Christ without preaching about Him? And how can we trust Him without being informed why and for what we are to trust Him?

The error to which I call attention does not consist in laying too much stress in teaching and believing the facts and doctrines of the Bible; but it consists in stopping short of trusting the personal Christ, only satisfying ourselves with believing the testimony concerning Him, thus resting in the belief of what God has said about Christ, rather than committing our souls to Him by an act of loving trust.

*F*ather, I thank you that love, joy and peace are all experiences of great blessing that you have bestowed upon me through the gift of your Holy Spirit in my life.

So many are missing them. I see Christians working in the Church who haven't experienced the love, joy and peace you want them to have, and they do not seem concerned about the work of the Holy Spirit in their lives or in the Church today. Help me, under the anointing of your spiritual power, to share with them the full gospel in a way that they will accept both you and your promises. Amen.

Every day will I praise you.

Psalm 145:2

23

All the Day—Every Day

*I*t is a step forward in the Christian life when you definitely decide to have fellowship with God in His Word each day without fail. Your perseverance will be crowned with success, if you are really serious about it. Your experience may be somewhat as follows.

On waking in the morning God will be your first thought. You must set apart a time for prayer and resolve to give God time to hear your requests and to reveal himself to you. Then you may speak out all your desires to God and expect an answer.

Later on in the day, even if only for a few minutes, you may take time to maintain your fellowship with God. And again in the evening, a quiet period will be necessary to review the day's work, remembering to confess any sins and receive the assurance of forgiveness, then dedicating yourself afresh to God and His service.

Such a person as this will gradually get an insight into what is lacking in his life, and will be ready to say, "Not only *every day* but *all the day*." He will realize that the Holy Spirit is in him unceasingly, just as his breathing is continuous. From the depths of his heart he will make it his aim to gain the assurance that God is with him all through the day.

All the day! Christian, the Holy Spirit says, "Today." "Behold, now is the accepted time!" A man who had undergone a serious operation asked the doctor, "How long will I have to lie here?" And the answer came, "Only one day at a time." And that is the law of the Christian life. God gave the manna daily, and the command to offer a morning and evening sacrifice on the altar—by these God showed that His children should live day by day.

Seek the leading of the Holy Spirit for the whole day. You need not worry about tomorrow, but rest in the assurance that He Who has led you today will draw still nearer tomorrow.

The Practice of Spiritual Power

It amazes me that the enduement of power from on high should be treated as of comparatively little importance. In theory it is admitted to be everything, but in practice it is treated as though it were nothing.

From the apostles to the present day, men of very little human culture, but endued with spiritual power, have been highly successful in winning souls to Christ, while some men of the greatest learning have been powerless as far as the work of the ministry is concerned. And yet we continue in this way, laying ten times more stress on human culture than we do on the baptism of the Holy Spirit, treating education as infinitely more important than the enduement of power from on high.

We must insist upon this enduement of power as indispensable to the work of the ministry. Believers must be given instruction in Christian spiritual experience. Christianity is an experience. Christianity is a consciousness, and personal fellowship with God is its secret.

This is where more training is needed. There is a world of essential learning in the direction of spiritual experience which is being wholly neglected. A genuine heart union with God and a prevailing with spiritual power with God and for souls is lacking. Too often, the least teaching is found in this area.

Dear God, I pray that there would be an increased study of your Word; not just for intellectual attainment, but for a deeper knowledge of you and greater spiritual attainment. Help all of us to manifest in our lives the power from on high that will lead others to seek you and seek more of you for the benefit of your growing kingdom on earth. Amen.

*T*he blood of Christ, who
through the eternal Spirit
offered himself unblemished
to God, cleanse our
consciences from acts that
lead to death so that we may
serve the living God.

Hebrews 9:14

24
The Spirit and the Cross

*T*he connection between the cross and the Spirit is inconceivably close and full of meaning. The Spirit brought Christ to the cross and enabled Him to die there. The cross was to Christ and to the Holy Spirit the culminating point of their desire on earth. The cross gave Christ the right to pray down the Holy Spirit on earth, because there He had made reconciliation for sin. The cross gave Christ the right and the power to grant us the power of the Spirit, because on it He freed us from the power of sin.

To put it briefly, Christ could not have attained to the heavenly life, or have poured out the Holy Spirit, if He had not first died to sin, to the world, and to His own life. He died to sin that He might live to God. And that is the way the Holy Spirit brings the cross into our hearts. It is only as those who have been crucified with Christ that we can receive the full power of the Spirit. It is because we do not realize how necessary it is to die to all earthly things that the Spirit cannot gain full possession of us.

Why do so few believers understand or experience that the fellowship of the Spirit is a fellowship of the cross? Simply because they do not feel the need of praying for the Spirit of wisdom to give them a deep, spiritual insight into the oneness of the Spirit and the cross. They try to use their human understanding, but there is too little waiting upon God to teach them divine truths through the Spirit.

My friend, begin asking God for the Spirit to take you to the cross of Christ, and in fellowship with Him die to the world and sin, so that all things may become new. If you will do this, you will actually live, walk, work and play in the Holy Spirit to the glory of God.

The Practice of Spiritual Power

Whenever we pray the "Lord's Prayer," we pray, "Thy will be done on earth as it is in heaven." God has not promised to hear *this* petition unless it is sincerely offered. But *sincerity* implies a state of mind that accepts the whole revealed will of God, so far as we understand it, as they accept it in heaven. It implies a loving, confiding, universal obedience to the whole *known* will of God, whether that will is revealed in His Word, by His Spirit, or in His providence. It implies that we hold ourselves and all that we have and are as absolutely and cordially at God's disposal as do the inhabitants of heaven. If we fall short of this, and withhold anything whatever from God, we "regard iniquity in our hearts," and God will not hear us.

Sincerity in offering this petition implies a state of entire and universal consecration to God. Anything short of this is withholding from God that which is His due. It is "turning away our ear from hearing the law." But what do the Scriptures say, "He that turneth away his ear from hearing the law, even his prayer shall be an abomination"? Do those who profess to be Christians understand this?

What is true of offering these two petitions is true of *all* prayer. All professed prayer is an abomination if it is not offered in a state of entire consecration of all that we have and are to God. If we do not offer ourselves with and in our prayers, with all that we have; if we are not in a state of mind that cordially accepts and, so far as we know, perfectly conforms to the whole will of God, our prayer is an abomination.

How awfully profane is the use very frequently made of the "Lord's Prayer" both in public and in private. To hear men and women chatter meaninglessly, "Thy kingdom come, Thy will be done on earth as it is in heaven," while their lives are anything but conformed to the known will of God is shocking and revolting. To hear men pray, "Thy kingdom come," while it is most evident that they are making little or no sacrifice or effort to promote this kingdom forces the conviction of barefaced hypocrisy. Such is not prevailing prayer.

*D*ear Father, give me such a vision of the cross, and such an understanding of Christ's death in behalf of sinners, that I will be willing to die to all selfishness within me. May everyone concerned with Christian faith begin to look to you for the enduement of spiritual power that enables you to build your house and convert souls to Christ. Anoint me that I might proclaim your gospel in a way that will lead others to fellowship with you. For the sake of Jesus' shed blood. Amen.

*T*here are three that testify: the Spirit, the water, and the blood; and the three are in agreement.

1 John 5:8

25
The Spirit and the Blood

*T*he water is external, a sign of the renewing and purifying through regeneration used in baptism. The Spirit and the blood are two spiritual expressions, working together in regeneration; the blood for the forgiveness of sins, the Spirit for the renewal of the whole nature. All through life the Spirit and the blood must agree.

Oneness in the Spirit and the blood is spiritual and true. Through the blood we obtain the Spirit, as through the blood we are redeemed and purified so as to receive the Spirit. Only through the blood can we with confidence pray for and receive the Spirit. Oh believer, if you would have boldness each day to trust to the guidance of the Holy Spirit, then let your faith in the precious blood be sure and strong.

There may be some sin in your life of which you are hardly conscious, but which grieves the Holy Spirit and drives Him away. The only way to avoid this is to believe that "the blood of Jesus Christ cleanses from all sin." Your only right to approach God is through the blood of the Lamb. Come with every sin, known or unknown, and plead the blood of Christ as your only claim on the love that accepts and forgives.

Nevertheless, do not rest content with the forgiveness of sins, but accept the fullness of the Holy Spirit to which the blood gives you access. In the Old Testament, the priest went into the Holy Place with the blood, and the high priest into the Holiest of All. Christ entered the heavenly sanctuary with His blood and poured out from there the Holy Spirit. Know that you have a right through the blood to the fullness of the Spirit.

As one who has been redeemed by the blood of Christ, make a complete surrender of yourself to God as His purchased possession, a vessel ready for Him to use, a dwelling place of the Holy Spirit.

The Practice of Spiritual Power

How can a sinner change his heart to attain righteousness? The Bible reveals the fact and human consciousness attests the truth that is necessary before the illumination of the Holy Spirit. A sinner can understand the claims of God, renounce selfishness and sympathize with God. A sinner attains, then, to righteousness only through the teachings and inspirations of the Holy Spirit.

This change from sin to righteousness must involve: (1) Confidence in God, or faith. Without confidence a person could not be persuaded to change his heart, to renounce self, and sympathize with God. (2) Repentance—the change of mind which consists in renunciation of self-seeking, and a coming into sympathy with God. (3) A radical change of moral attitude with respect to God and our neighbor.

All these are involved in a change of heart. They occur simultaneously, and the presence of one implies the existence and presence of the others. It is by the truths of the gospel that the Holy Spirit brings this change in sinful man. This revelation of divine love, when powerfully sent home by the Holy Spirit, is what changes sinners.

Righteousness is then sustained in the human soul by the indwelling of Christ through faith and in no other way. It cannot be sustained by purposes or resolutions self-originated. Only Christ himself produces righteousness. Through faith, Christ first gains ascendency in the human heart, and through faith He maintains this ascendancy and reigns as king in the soul.

All outward conformity to the law and commandments of God that does not proceed from Christ working in the soul by His Holy Spirit is self-righteousness. All true righteousness, then, is the righteousness of faith, or a righteousness secured by Christ through faith in Him.

*D*ear Father, I continue to pray for a deeper work of your Spirit in my life. Help me to bear the fruits of the Spirit when I judge the state of the Church and the world according to your holy standards. May the blood of Christ cleanse us from all wrongdoing, and the Holy Spirit empower us to do what is right. For Jesus' sake. Amen.

*Our gospel came to you
. . . with power, with the
Holy Spirit, and with deep
conviction. . . . You
welcomed the message with
the joy given by the Holy
Spirit.*

1 Thessalonians 1:5, 6

26
The Spirit in Preacher and Hearer

*P*aul more than once reminds his converts that the chief characteristic of his preaching was *the power—the supernatural power of the Holy Spirit.* To the Corinthians he wrote, "And my speech and my preaching was not with enticing words of man's wisdom, but in demonstration of the Spirit and of power: That your faith should not stand in the wisdom of men, but in the power of God" (1 Corinthians 2:4, 5). The Holy Spirit was so imparted to his hearers that they received the Word "with joy of the Holy Spirit."

This is one of the most important lessons in the spiritual life. We, as hearers, are so accustomed to listen attentively to the sermon to see what it has to teach us that we are apt to forget that the blessing of our church-going depends on our doing two things. First, praying for the preacher that he may speak "in the demonstration of the Spirit and of power." Second, praying for the congregation and for ourselves that we may receive God's Word, "which effectually worketh also in you that believe" (1 Thessalonians 2:13).

Often there is no manifestation of the Spirit because both the speaking and the hearing are the work of human understanding or feeling. Often there is no power that raises the soul with spiritual insight into the life of faith that God has provided for His children.

How earnestly we should pray for God to reveal to us all *the Spirit of wisdom and revelation* that we may discover what the place really is that the Holy Spirit should have in our lives, and what the perfect work is that He will do within us! God help us to learn this prayer! Then we shall understand what Christ meant when He told His disciples to wait for the power of the Spirit, and then "ye shall be My witnesses . . . unto the uttermost part of the earth" (Acts 1:48).

Pray earnestly that God may teach us to pray down the power of the Holy Spirit upon ministers and missionaries and their congregations, that the preaching may be in the manifestation of the Spirit and of power for the conversion and sanctification of souls.

The Practice of Spiritual Power

Prevailing prayer secures an answer. Saying prayers is not offering prevailing prayer. The prevailing prayer does not depend so much on quantity as on quality. The best way to approach this subject is by relating an experience I had before I was converted. I relate it because I fear such experiences are all too common among unconverted people.

I do not remember ever attending a prayer meeting until after I began studying law. Then, for the first time, I lived in a neighborhood where there was a weekly prayer meeting. I had neither known, heard, nor seen much of religion; hence, I had no settled opinion about it. Partly from curiosity and partly from an uneasiness of mind upon the subject, which I could not well define, I began to attend that prayer meeting. About the same time I bought the first Bible I ever owned and began to read it. I listened to the prayers that I heard offered in those prayer meetings with all the attention I could give to prayers so cold and formal. In every prayer they prayed for the gift and out-pouring of the Holy Spirit. Both in their prayers and in their remarks they acknowledged that they did not prevail with God. This was most evident and almost made me a skeptic.

Seeing me so frequently in their prayer meeting, the leader on one occasion asked me if I wanted them to pray for me. I replied, "No. I suppose that I need to be prayed for, but your prayers are not answered. You confess it yourselves." I then expressed my astonishment at this fact in view of what the Bible said about prevailing prayer. Indeed, because of this my mind was very troubled and began doubting Christ's teaching on the subject of prayer.

Was Christ a divine teacher? Did He actually teach what the gospels attributed to Him? Did He mean what He said? Did prayer really work to secure blessings from God? If so, what was I to make of what I witnessed from week to week and month to month in that prayer meeting? Were they real Christians? Was that which I heard *real prayer*, in the Bible sense? Was it such prayer as Christ had promised to answer?

*D*ear Father, the prayers of the Church have been so feeble, because the faith of Christians has been so weak. How often have we actually led people into everlasting skepticism because we have been so ineffective in our prayers? Forgive us for the times we have not prevailed in prayer simply because we have not in faith fulfilled the conditions that you have set forth in Scripture to answer our prayers. In the days ahead, increase my knowledge and my faith regarding what you want to do in my life and in the life of your Church in answer to prayer. Amen.

*T*hen Peter said: Repent
. . . that your sins may be
forgiven. You will receive
the gift of the Holy Spirit.

Acts 2:38

27

The Full Gospel

When John the Baptist preached, "Repent ye, for the kingdom of heaven is at hand," he also said, "He that cometh after me . . . shall baptize you with the Holy Spirit and with fire." When Christ preached the gospel of the kingdom He said, "There be some of them that stand here which shall not taste of death, till they have seen the kingdom of God come with power." This is what happened at the outpouring of the Holy Spirit. On the Day of Pentecost, Peter preached the full gospel of repentance and forgiveness of sins, *and the gift of the Holy Spirit.* This is indispensable in preaching the gospel, for then only is it possible for a believer to live in the will of God and to please Him in all things. The kingdom of God is righteousness (in Christ), and joy (in God) through the Holy Spirit. The continuous joy of which Christ speaks, "My joy," can only be obtained through the power of the Holy Spirit.

How often only half the gospel is preached—conversion and forgiveness of sins—and souls are led no further into the truth. The knowledge and appropriation of the life of the Holy Spirit within us is not mentioned. No wonder that so many Christians fail to understand that they must depend each day on the Spirit for the joy which will be their strength.

Dear Christian, accept this truth for yourself, as well as for those among whom you labor—*that the daily enjoyment of the leading of God's Spirit is necessary for a joyous life of faith*. If you feel that there has been a lack in your spiritual life, then begin at once to pray to the Father to grant you the gift of the Holy Spirit anew each day. Then trust yourself to His leading and guidance all the day. Let the remembrance of the text in Galatians 5:22–23 give you courage for all that the Holy Spirit will do for you: "The fruit of the Spirit is love, joy, peace, long-suffering, gentleness, goodness, faith, meekness, temperance."

Regard your heart constantly as a garden for the Lord in which the Holy Spirit will bear abundant fruit to the glory of God.

The Practice of Spiritual Power

After attending the prayer meeting I mentioned earlier, I came to the conclusion that those praying were under a delusion. They did not prevail because they had no *right* to prevail. They did not comply with the conditions upon which God had promised to hear prayer. Their prayers were just such as God had promised *not* to answer. It was evident they were overlooking the fact that they were in danger of praying themselves into skepticism in regard to the value of prayer.

In reading my Bible, I noticed such revealed conditions as the following:

1. Faith in God as the Answerer of prayer. This, it is plain, involves the expectation of receiving what we ask.

2. Another revealed condition is asking according to

the revealed will of God. This plainly implies asking not only for such things as God is willing to grant, but also asking in such a state of mind as God can accept. I fear it is common for people who profess to be believers to overlook the state of mind in which God requires them to be as a condition for answering their prayers.

For example: In offering the Lord's Prayer, "Thy kingdom come," it is plain that sincerity is a condition of prevailing with God. But sincerity in offering this petition implies the thorough consecration of all that we have and all that we are to the building up of Christ's kingdom. To utter this petition in any other state of mind involves hypocrisy and is an abomination.

Lord Jesus, help us to work with everyone in the Church in such a way that we can help them see beyond repentance and baptism to receiving the gift of the Holy Spirit in power. Help us to examine carefully and explain to others the conditions that you have set forth to answer our prayers. Help us to see what it must mean for us personally to really pray, "Thy kingdom come," so these words will not just be so much formality in public settings. O Lord, we really do want your will to be done and your kingdom to come. Show us what this means in the situations we find ourselves in so that we can pray according to your will. Amen.

You are a letter from Christ, the result of our ministry, written not with ink but with the Spirit of the living God, not on tablets of stone but on tablets of human hearts.

2 Corinthians 3:3

28
The Ministry of the Spirit

*T*he Corinthian Church was a "letter of recommendation" for Paul showing how much he had done for them. Although he claimed nothing for himself, God had enabled him as a "minister of the Spirit" to write in their hearts "with the Spirit of the living God." He himself declared: "Not that we are sufficient of ourselves to think anything as of ourselves; but our sufficiency is of God; who also hath made us able ministers of the New Testament."

Only through the power of the Holy Spirit is a preacher able to be a minister of the Spirit, with power to write in the hearts of his people the name and the love of Christ. What a wonderful testimony to have! No wonder that when speaking of the glory that was upon the face of Moses when he communed with God, Paul says, the ministry of the Spirit is more glorious "by reason of the glory that excelleth." He then speaks of how "we all, with open face beholding as in a glass the glory of the Lord, are changed into the same image from glory into glory, even as by the Spirit of the Lord."

Oh, that God would restore the ministry of the gospel to its original power! Oh, that all ministers and church members would unite in prayer that God, by the mighty working of His Spirit, would give the ministry of the Holy Spirit His rightful place and teach the people to believe that when Christ is preached to them they are beholding as in a glass the glory of the Lord and may be changed into the same image by the Spirit of the Lord!

What a call that is for us to persevere in prayer that the Holy Spirit may again have His rightful place in the ministry of the Word so that the exceeding and abundant glory of this ministry may be manifested.

The Practice of Spiritual Power

If any of the early believers, to whom the commandment to be filled with the Spirit was given, had failed to receive spiritual power, should we not think they were greatly to blame? And if it had been sin in them, how much more in us with all the light of history and of fact blazing upon us, which they had not received!

Some ministers and many Christians treat this matter as if it were to be left to the [arbitrary] sovereignty of God, without the need of any persistent effort to obtain this enduement. Did the early believers so understand and treat it? No, indeed. They gave themselves no rest until this baptism of power came upon them.

I once heard a minister preaching upon the subject of the baptism of the Holy Spirit. He treated it as a reality. And when he came to the question of how it was to be obtained, he said truly it was to be obtained as the apostles obtained it at Pentecost. I was much gratified, and I listened eagerly to hear him press the obligation on his listeners to give themselves no rest until they had obtained it.

130

The apostles did not try to embrace the baptism of the Holy Spirit with their intellects *before* they embraced it with their hearts. They believed the Word of God through Christ. It was with them, as it should be with us, a question of *faith* in a *promise from a trustworthy God*. I find many people endeavoring to grasp with their intellect and settle as a theory questions of pure experience. They are puzzling themselves with endeavors to apprehend with the intellect that which is to be received as a conscious experience through faith in the living God.

Dear Jesus, the Church for too long has not consecrated herself wholly to serving you and the world you died to save. We have continued to feed a body that exists more for itself than for you and others. I am a part of that Church. Her failings are my own failings as well. Help every Christian to consecrate himself or herself wholly to doing your will with the desire that your kingdom might really come. Help us to make a difference in the Church, and help the Church to make a difference in the world in which we live. Amen.

Those who have preached the gospel to you by the Holy Spirit sent from heaven.

1 Peter 1:12

29
The Spirit From Heaven

Christ has taught us to think of God as our own Father in heaven, who is ready to bestow His blessings on His children on earth. Our Lord himself was taken up into the glory of heaven, and we are told that we are seated with Him in the heavenly places in Christ. The Holy Spirit comes to us from heaven to pour into our hearts all the light and the love and the joy and the power of heaven.

Those who are truly filled with the Holy Spirit have a heavenly life in themselves. Their walk and conversation are in heaven. They are in daily fellowship with the Father and with the Son. They seek the things that are above, for their life is hid with Christ in God. Their chief characteristic is heavenly-mindedness. They carry about with them the marks of their eternal, heavenly destiny.

How can one cultivate this heavenly disposition? By allowing the Holy Spirit sent from heaven to do His heavenly work in our hearts, and bring to maturity the fruits of the Spirit which grow in the Paradise of God. The Holy

Spirit will raise our hearts daily to fellowship with God in heaven, and will teach us to dwell in the heavenlies with Him. The Spirit makes the glorified Christ in heaven present in our hearts and teaches us to dwell in His abiding presence.

Oh Christian, take time each day to receive from the Father the continual guidance of the Holy Spirit. Let Him overcome the world for you, and strengthen you as a child of heaven to walk daily with your God and with the Lord Jesus. Do not be unbelieving. The Holy Spirit will do His part, if you in faith surrender yourself to His control. You will learn to speak to others with such heavenly joy that you will draw them to give themselves to the leading of the Holy Spirit and to walk in the heavenly joy of Christ's love.

The Practice of Spiritual Power

Some have maintained that we should conform to the ways of the world somewhat—at least enough to show that we can enjoy the world and Jesus too—and that we make Christianity appear repulsive to unconverted souls by turning our backs upon their amusements. But we should represent Christianity as it really is—as living above the world, as consisting in a heavenly mind, as that which affords an enjoyment so spiritual and heavenly as to render the low pursuits and joys of worldly people disagreeable and repulsive. It is a sad stumbling block to the unconverted to see professed believers seeking their pleasure and happiness from this world's ways. Such pleasure seeking misrepresents Jesus. It misleads, bewilders, and confuses the observing outsider. If he ever reads the Bible, he cannot but wonder that souls who are born of God and have communion with Him should have any relish for worldly ways and pleasures. Thoughtful, unconverted people have little or no confidence in professing believers who seek enjoyment from worldly pleasures.

Believers should live so far above the world as not to need or seek worldly pleasures, and thus commend Christianity to the world as a source of the highest and purest happiness. The peaceful look, the joyful countenance, the spiritual serenity and cheerfulness of living the Christian life recommends the Christian faith to the unconverted. Their satisfaction in God, their holy joy, their living above and shunning the ways of worldly minds, impress the unconverted with a sense of the necessity and desirableness of a Christian life. Let no one think to gain a really Christian influence over another by manifesting a sympathy with his worldly aspirations.

*D*ear Father, you have made everything available to your Church. You have given your Son, who died for her. You have given your Spirit to cleanse her and guide her, to empower her for service. You have given her your Holy Word of truth to answer the deepest questions of the longing heart. You have made Christ the head over all powers and authorities. I praise you, Father, for these manifold gifts that make being in your presence the joy of my life. Help me to fulfill the conditions of prevailing prayer always, that nothing would corrupt my relationship with you. Amen.

I tell you the truth, my
Father will give you
whatever you ask in my
name.

John 16:23

30
The Spirit and Prayer

*I*n our Lord's farewell discourse reported in John chapters 13–17, Jesus presented life in the dispensation of the Holy Spirit in all its power and attractiveness. One of the most glorious results of the day when the Holy Spirit should come would be *the new power that we should have* to pray down from heaven the power of God to bless the world. Seven times we have the promise repeated: *Whatsoever ye shall ask* IN MY NAME, *that will I do* (see John 14:13, 14; 15:7, 16; 16:23, 24, 26). Study these passages that you may come to understand fully how urgently and earnestly our Lord repeated the promise.

In the power of the perfect salvation that Christ accomplished, in the power of His glory with the Father, in the power of the outpouring of the Holy Spirit, dwelling in the hearts of His children, believers have the marvelous freedom to ask what they desired of the fullness of the will of God, and it should be done. Everything was included in these few words: *Whatsover ye shall ask in my name, that will I do.*

During the ten days before Pentecost, the disciples put this promise to the test. In response to their continuous united prayer, the heavens were opened and the Spirit of God descended to earth to dwell in their hearts, filling them with His life-power. They received the power of the Spirit that they might impart it to thousands. That power is still *the pledge for all time of what God will do*. If God's children will agree with one accord to wait for the promise of the Father each day, there is no limit to what God will do for them.

Oh believer, remember that you are living in the dispensation of the Holy Spirit. That means that the Holy Spirit will dwell in you with heavenly power, enabling you to testify for Him. But it also means that you may unite with God's children to ask in prayer greater and more wonderful things than the heart has conceived.

The Practice of Spiritual Power

We must evaluate our prayer lives to see if we are meeting these conditions of prevailing prayer:

1. *The inspiration of the Holy Spirit.* All truly prevailing prayer is inspired by the Holy Spirit. "For we know not what we should pray for as we ought, but the Spirit itself maketh intercession for us with the groanings which cannot be uttered. And He that searcheth the hearts knoweth what is the mind of the Spirit, because He maketh intercession for the saints according to the will of God" (Romans 8:26, 27). This is the true spirit of prayer. This is being led by the Spirit in prayer. It is the only really prevailing prayer. Unless believers are taught how to pray by the intercession of the Spirit in them, they cannot prevail with God.

2. *Fervency.* A prayer, to be prevailing, must be fervent. "Confess your faults one to another, and pray one for another, that ye may be healed. The effectual fervent prayer of a righteous man availeth much" (James 5:16).

3. *Perseverance or persistence in prayer.* See the cases of

Jacob, of Daniel, of Elijah, of the Syrophoenecian woman, of the unjust judge, and the teaching of the Bible generally.

4. *Travail of soul.* "As soon as Zion travailed, she brought forth her children." "My little children," said Paul, "of whom I travail in birth again, till Christ be formed in you." This implies that he had travailed in birth for them before they were converted. Indeed, travail of soul in prayer is the only real revival prayer. If anyone does not know what this is, he does not understand the spirit of prayer. He is not in a revival state. Until he understands this agonizing prayer, he does not know the real secret of revival power.

5. *Specific prevailing prayer.* It is offered for a definite object. We cannot prevail for everything at once. In all the cases recorded in the Bible in which prayer was answered, it is noteworthy that the petitioner prayed for a definite object.

6. *Meaning what we say.* We make no false pretences; in short, that we are entirely childlike and sincere, speaking out of the heart, nothing more nor less than what we mean, feel and believe.

7. *Believing the good faith of God to keep all His promises.*

8. *Guarding against everything that can quench or grieve the Spirit of God in our hearts.* We must watch for the answer in a state of mind that will diligently use all necessary means, at any expense, and add entreaty to entreaty.

*F*ather, help me to offer more effective prayers to you. Help me to keep up a close relationship with you so prayer is never mechanical, and so I never think that prayer is to manipulate you. May your Word and Holy Spirit teach me how to pray and prevail for Jesus' sake. Amen.

*T*hey all joined together constantly in prayer. When the day of Pentecost came . . . all of them were filled with the Holy Spirit.

Acts 1:14; 2:1, 4

31
With One Accord in Prayer

Our Lord gave the command to His disciples: "Go ye into all the world and preach the gospel to every creature," and He added the promise: "Lo, I am with you always." We may be fully assured that this command and this promise were not meant for the disciples alone, *but also for us.*

Just before His ascension, Christ gave His very last command, also with a promise attached to it. The command was: "Do not leave . . . wait for the gift my Father promised." And the promise was: "Ye shall receive power after that the Holy Spirit is come upon you; and ye shall be witnesses unto Me . . . unto the uttermost part of the earth." *This very command and promise are also meant for us.*

For ten days the disciples pled that promise with one accord, and their prayer was wonderfully answered. Unfortunately, the Church of our day has failed along these lines. It has tried to carry out the first command, "Preach the gospel"; but has often forgotten the second, "Wait for the promise of the Father." The call comes to each believer to *pray daily with one accord* for this great gift of the Holy Spirit. Many Christians pray for themselves and their own work, but forget to pray for the Church of Christ. The power of the first disciples lay in the fact that they *as one Body* were prepared to forget themselves and instead pray for the Holy Spirit over all mankind.

Oh believer, whatever you may have learned from reading this little book, learn one more lesson. *Daily prayer in fellowship with God's children is indispensable*, and it is a sacred duty if the Spirit is going to come again in power. Don't let your prayers for the working of God's Holy Spirit be limited to yourself alone, nor even to your congregation, but in a world-embracing love of Christ, pray that all God's children and His kingdom over the whole world will be filled with power from on high.

The Practice of Spiritual Power

To pray for revival, and use no other means to bring it about, is to tempt God. This, I could plainly see, was the case of those who offered prayer in the prayer meeting mentioned earlier. They continued praying for revival, but after the meeting they were as silent as death on the subject and opened not their mouths to those around them.

They continued this inconsistency until a prominent unrepentant man in the community administered to them in my presence a terrible rebuke. He expressed just what I deeply felt. He rose, and with the utmost solemnity and tearfulness said: "Christian people, what can you mean? You continue to pray in these meetings for a revival of religion. You often exhort each other here to wake up and use means to promote a revival. You assure one another, and assure us who are unrepentant, that we are on the way to hell; and I believe it. You also insist that if you should wake up, and use the appropriate means, there would be a revival and we should be converted. You tell us of our great danger, and that our souls are worth more than all worlds; and yet you keep about your comparatively trifling employments and use no such means. We have no revival and our souls are not saved." Here he broke down and fell, sobbing, back into his seat.

This rebuke fell heavily upon that prayer meeting. It did them good; for it was not long before the members of that prayer meeting broke down and we had a revival. I was present in the first meeting in which the revival spirit was manifest. Oh! How changed was the tone of their prayers, confessions and supplications. In returning home, I remarked to a friend: "What a change has come over these Christians. This must be the beginning of a revival." Yes. A wonderful change comes over all meetings whenever the Christian people are revived. Then their confessions mean something. They mean reformation and restitution. They mean work. They open their pockets, their hearts and hands, and the devotion of all their powers to the promotion of the work.

Dear Father God, Lord Jesus Christ, Holy Spirit, come into my life with power today. Fill me with your presence that I might bear the fruits of the Holy Spirit and manifest the gifts of the Holy Spirit in such a way that people can see the divine truth of the Scriptures and commit their lives totally and unreservedly to you and your kingdom. I pray there might be revival in your Church and the conversion of many. Help believers everywhere to be faithful in their prayer life and work for you, because they truly love you with all their heart and mind and soul and strength. Come quickly, Lord Jesus. Amen.